Amelia Earhart

Amelia Earhart

IMAGE AND ICON

EDITED BY KRISTEN LUBBEN AND ERIN BARNETT

WITH ESSAYS BY KRISTEN LUBBEN, SUSAN BUTLER, AND SUSAN WARE

International Center of Photography

STEIDL

Contents

Director's Foreword

Seventy years after her disappearance, Amelia Earhart remains one of the most celebrated women of the twentieth century. Fascination with her and her brief but influential life has persisted since 1928, when she was the first woman to fly across the Atlantic. Today her photographic image is a virtual sign for convention-defying womanhood. How do such celebrity photographs construct meaning? How does an individual navigate and manipulate his or her own public image? And how are such representations—or misrepresentations—fostered and disseminated by the mass media? *Amelia Earhart: Image and Icon* takes famed American aviator Amelia Earhart as a case study to examine the essential role that photography plays in the creation of fame and its cultural impact.

Certainly fashionable portraits by well-known society photographers such as Edward Steichen contributed to the construction of Earhart's singular image. But even more influential were the contributions of thousands of anonymous or little-known press photographers. Their innumerable images shaped how the public perceived not just Earhart herself, but the possibilities for women and the relatively new technology of flight. From its inception, ICP has been committed to understanding the impact of photojournalism. Tracing the development and consolidation of Earhart's image through studio portraits, advertisements, newspaper coverage, women's magazines, and more provides a lens onto the practical applications and the distribution of photographs during a period of revolutionary change in the print media.

Earhart's fame spanned the years 1928 to 1937, a period of dramatic proliferation of the illustrated press, and the fortunes of the two were interrelated. Portraits of celebrities like Earhart leavened the news and sold papers and magazines, and the fame that such coverage afforded Earhart allowed her to fund her flying. In recent years, ICP has explored the history of photography in print through a number of exhibitions, including *The Rise of the Picture Press, Picturing Business: The Photography of Fortune,* and *Looking at LIFE.* This project adds to that inquiry, through an examination of the representation of one individual across a variety of print sources. Focusing on the history of photographs in print sheds light on their reception and circulation, and on how images become part of a shared understanding of history.

The Amelia Earhart exhibition—and this publication, which accompanies it—would not have been possible without the help of many individuals. For bringing the rich possibility of exploring photographs of Earhart to our attention, we thank Ann Lawrence Morse and Susan Butler. Ms. Butler also contributed a biographical portrait of Earhart to this volume, drawn from *East to the Dawn,* her authoritative biography. Historian Susan Ware kindly allowed us to publish a chapter from her examination of Earhart's relationship to women's lives in the 1920s and '30s, *Still Missing: Amelia Earhart and the Search for Modern Feminism*. ICP Publications Committee co-chairs Frank Arisman and Andrew Lewin were also pivotal in helping this project take flight, as were their fellow committee members. Associate Curator Kristen Lubben and Assistant Curator Erin Barnett, who curated the exhibition and edited this volume, revealed a new lens through which to understand a familiar cultural icon; Ms. Lubben contributed further context in her essay on Earhart and the image of the New Woman. Brian Wallis, Director of Exhibitions and Chief Curator, provided essential insight that helped the project take form. Director of Publications Karen Hansgen deftly saw this catalogue through its many stages of development, with the assistance of Elizabeth Van Meter. Imaging technician Christopher George scanned many of the photographs and ephemera reproduced in the catalogue. Rhys Conlon, Minjung Lee, and Laura Diamond contributed indispensable research assistance, and interns Ana Cho, Emily Bierman, and Stefanie Petrilli aided in many stages of the project. For her intelligent and careful attention to the catalogue text, thanks to editor Philomena Mariani. Gerhard Steidl and his staff are responsible for the superb printing and production of this book. Amy Kleppner kindly lent her support to this endeavor, as did Richard S. and Margaret B. Patton, Adden B. Chrystie, and Alice Chrystie Wyman. For assistance with loans, rights, and research, we are grateful to: Nancy Lee and Jim Mones, New York Times; Kathi Doak and Regina Feiler, Time, Inc.; Diana Carey and Katherine Kraft, The Schlesinger Library, Radcliffe Institute, Harvard University; Frank Goodyear, National Portrait Gallery; Gretchen Fenston and Leigh Montville, Conde Nast; Sammie Morris, Purdue University Libraries; Melissa Kaiser, National Air and Space Museum; James Zeender, National Archives; Ray Chipault, Underwood Archives, Inc.; Laura Smith, George Eastman House; Jeremy McGraw, New York Public Library, Billy Rose Theater Collection; Sue Pinchot; Herbert Keppler; Lucy von Brachel, The Metropolitan Museum of Art; Eva Tucholka, Culver Pictures, Inc.

The exhibition that this catalogue accompanies is made possible with support from Ann L. Morse, Frank and Mary Ann Arisman, Thomas L. Chrystie and Eliza B. Chrystie, Andrew and Marina Lewin, and other donors.

Willis E. Hartshorn
Ehrenkranz Director

Fame, Flight, and the New Woman:

Photographs of Amelia Earhart

Kristen Lubben

Amelia Earhart is among those rare celebrities who are as familiar today as they were in their own time. Photographs of the iconic aviator, with tousled hair, leather jacket, and silk scarf, helped to secure her fame and ensure its perpetuation. Her disappearance over the Pacific Ocean in 1937 is undeniably part of the story; the dramatic and unsolved circumstances of her demise, and the lack of physical evidence, are powerful factors that contribute to keeping her image alive in the popular consciousness, and the trope of the popular hero who dies dramatically at the height of fame is a familiar one. However, her end does not explain the appeal of her image in her own time—particularly to women—or its continued currency as shorthand for a range of cultural and stylistic ideals today.

Two ad campaigns from the 1990s make clear that Earhart's image continues to represent much more than her spectacular finish. In the late 1990s, Apple launched its "Think Different" campaign: a series of magazine ads, billboards, and posters with a single black-and-white portrait of an iconic innovator, along with the Apple logo and the tagline "Think Different," an attempt to underscore Apple's position as rebel to IBM's mainstream (whose longtime slogan was "Think"), and to associate the brand with creative risk-takers. Along with images of Gandhi, Albert Einstein, and Miles Davis, Apple employed an early portrait of Earhart. It shows her in white flying helmet with goggles perched on her head. Her white shirt and tie are out of focus, so that the suggestion of menswear is present without being foregrounded, and creates a foil for her model-like looks, youthfulness, and femininity. Her expression is both doe-eyed and determined. Earhart's image needs no caption: it is understood that the viewer will recognize her, and will associate the Apple brand with daring and adventure, as well as unconventionality, conveyed by the gender-bending signals in the portrait. In a similar campaign by Gap in 1993, the company employed a series of American icons to sell khaki pants. The photograph of Earhart selected for this campaign shows the aviator (in khakis) next to her plane. Her mastery of the machine that dwarfs her in the photograph telegraphs her confidence and modernity, while her boyish, almost childish demeanor disarms and lends her an air of vulnerability.[1] Both ads rest almost solely on the array of associations with Earhart's photographic image, identifiable and potent enough to sell clothes and computers seventy years after her disappearance.

In her own time, Earhart was appealing because she represented the physical embodiment of heady new ideals circulating in the culture. Chief among these was the figure of the New Woman, an independent and convention-defying version of modern womanhood. She represented a break with the nineteenth-century cult of domesticity and True Womanhood symbolized by "the angel in the house," a woman devoted to the exclusively female sphere of home and childrearing, and who by her example reinforced the moral code. The New Woman emerged in the 1890s, and remained a source of both fascination and anxiety as her image evolved through the early decades of the twentieth century. Earhart, a career woman not subservient to her husband, an athlete, and an active participant in the national project of progress and modernity, exemplified a particular version of the New Woman. She also represented, whether by design or synchronicity, a physical style that reflected the changing fashion in clothing and body type in the 1920s and '30s. She was in sync with styles promoted by Hollywood and fashion designers, in her thinness, androgyny, short hair, and even sunned skin. An outspoken advocate of women's rights in the postsuffrage era, she offered women a new, seemingly more modern feminist model, one which did not look like the matronly older generation of suffragette activists. Above all else, her profession endowed her with its aura of excitement, advancement, and risk. In an era before commercial aviation, the aviator was a heroic symbol of modernism. His female counterpart, the aviatrix, was the ultimate glamorous and daring modern woman, able to employ technology to transcend the limitations of body, gender, and tradition. Earhart stepped into the stylistic template established by other female flyers, beginning with Harriet Quimby, Katherine Stinson, and others as early as the teens. But while Earhart's image incorporated existing iconography, it was also essentially authentic: like her name—almost too good to be true—her leather jacket, short hair, and other key elements of her signature style were not the constructions of a publicist but perfected, refined versions of her own (prefame) self-presentation.[2]

The many photographs taken of Earhart demonstrate that, in the words of one biographer, she had an "unerring instinct for making a physical statement of who and what she was."[3] The complex cultural and stylistic ideals that she embodied are conveyed in even relatively straightforward portraits. However, in their original contexts, the photographs also reveal the ways in which this potent image was threatening and required management or mediation, whether within the photographic image itself or through the framing devices of layout, picture selection, and captioning.

From the outset, Earhart's image was entangled with the struggle over the representation of American womanhood. She was launched to sudden celebrity in 1928, when she was invited to become the first woman to cross the Atlantic in an airplane. The flight was the brain child of Amy Guest, an American-born British socialite who had intended to make the flight herself until her family balked. Spurring Guest on was the desire to prevent Mabel Boll, another American flyer, from making the Atlantic crossing. Dubbed the "Queen of Diamonds" by the press because of her fondness for decking herself out in jewels, Boll was deemed an unseemly, publicity-hungry adventuress by Guest. Guest was determined to bankroll the project with a more "suitable" representative of American womanhood and enlisted the aid of U.S.-based promoters, including George Palmer Putnam, a publisher who had capitalized on the excitement surrounding Charles Lindbergh's solo Atlantic crossing the year before. Putnam and his colleagues were told to look for "someone nice who will do us proud." After considering a number of high-profile female aviators, they were referred to Earhart, "a young social worker who flies."[4] *New York Times* correspondent Hilton H. Railey recalled, "Mrs. Guest had stipulated the person to whom she would yield must be 'representative' of American women. In Amelia Earhart I saw not only their norm but their sublimation."[5] The tall and slender Earhart impressed the search committee with her physical appearance as well as her modesty, wholesomeness, and genuine interest in flight; she was both attractive and the "right sort of girl." Not incidentally, they were struck by Earhart's similarities to Lindbergh, which Putnam no doubt recognized he could exploit as a promotional angle. Without interviewing any other candidates, they offered the opportunity to Earhart and she quickly accepted.

Plans for the flight were kept under wraps—not even Earhart's mother was informed—so that Boll would not move up her intended departure date. While waiting in Boston for the plane to be readied, Putnam arranged for a secret portrait session. On the roof of the Copley Plaza Hotel, where Earhart was staying, Paramount photographer Jake Coolidge supervised a photo session themed "Remember Lindbergh," in which Earhart wore her leather jacket, lace-up boots, and flying helmet. Claiming that the famous resemblance had more to do with his photographic skills than serendipity, Coolidge later said, "It wasn't so much that the resemblance was there as that you could make it seem to be there, by camera angles."[6] The photographs were widely circulated with captions that drew attention to the physical similarities between the two flyers, earning Earhart the tag "Lady Lindy," which, to her frustration, stuck throughout her career. Historian Susan Ware points out that the "nickname . . . had chauvinistic overtones, for it suggested that her feats were most important when linked to, or reflective of, his."[7] However, the two do indeed share interesting similarities, which serve to explain their appeal. In addition to their height, slender build, tousled light hair, and youthful appearance, Lindbergh and Earhart were both modest, temperate Midwesterners. As Charles L. Ponce de Leon argues, a subtext of Lindbergh's appeal was a rejection of the "urban and ethnic cultural styles" represented by such popular 1920s figures as Jack Dempsey and Babe Ruth, seen as flamboyant and swaggering compared with Lindbergh's reserve. "By the early 1930s, the jazz age would be reviled as a mindless, wasteful debauch, and spokesmen for the dominant culture would be hard at work trying to kindle public interest in national symbols that bore no trace of the booster spirit of the 1920s. Lindbergh was the first of such symbols."[8] Earhart, too, was understood as a counter to the media-hyped image of the flapper, that icon of the '20s, and anticipated the more serious and conservative mood of the 1930s.[9] In a November 1928 article in *Cosmopolitan* magazine entitled "I Want You to Meet a Real American Girl," O. O. McIntyre hailed the coming transformation:

. . . for a number of years youth has stampeded the conventions and gone on a bust. I have myself beheld gradual stages of decadence—from sly gin-guzzling to a calculated harlotry—among those fresh and vibrant young girls reared in a careful luxury. . . . I believe America's proud and convincing answer to it all is Amelia Earhart! . . . Hers is the healthy curiosity of the clean mind and the strong body and a challenging rebuke to those of us who have damned the youth of the land. To few generations have come a Lindbergh and an Amelia Earhart and their coming is a singular and welcome proof of our destiny. A generation producing them has no need to worry about its flappers and cake eaters. . . . Amelia Earhart becomes to all of us one of the significant figures of our time. Not only because she has accomplished what no other woman has accomplished but because she has provided an intellectual, courageous and highly moral reaction from the inflamed tendencies and appetites which have aroused so much alarm. She will become a symbol of new womanhood—a symbol, I predict, that will be emulously patterned after by thousands of young girls in their quest of the Ideal. What a girl!

Prior to the transatlantic flight, the *New York Times* for June 4, 1928, ran two photographs under the headline "Boston Girl Starts for Atlantic Hop." In one, the fresh-faced "Boston Girl" (who was, in fact, a thirty-year-old native Kansan) is seated on a windowsill, hands demurely crossed in her lap, wearing a dress that looks like a child's sailor suit or school uniform. The other is a full-length portrait from the "Lady Lindy" session. The photographs can read as "before and after" shots—documenting the moment when Earhart is plucked from obscurity and recreated as a famous aviator. But they also establish what becomes a convention in the layout of photographs of Earhart. Particularly in her early career, she is rarely represented by just one image; most often, a picture of the leather-and-pants-clad aviator is paired with one of Earhart in a dress, reminding the viewer that her identity as aviator is a costume that can be removed at will, and that her femininity remains secure.

Although Earhart was already an accomplished flyer, having bought her first plane five years earlier, she did none of the actual flying on the 1928 trip. Nonetheless, she was of far more interest to the press than her crewmates, Lou Gordon and Wilmer Stultz. She was celebrated upon landing in London, and the press eagerly followed her tour of the city. Reinforcing her image as a modest young woman, photographs of her in ill-fitting dresses carried captions explaining that she had to borrow clothes from friends in London because she was so sensible and lacking in vanity that she wore only her flight suit on the trip, and did not pack a change of clothes for fear of adding more weight to the plane. (Throughout her career, modesty and seriousness of purpose were used to explain her unfeminine appearance.) Another article notes that in the loaned frocks Earhart "was suddenly and miraculously transformed from a daring celebrated aviatrix to a typical, nice American girl having a celebration abroad with a party of friends from home."[10] Earhart returned to parades and accolades in America. Overnight, she had become a media star.

Fame preempted her plans to resume life at the Boston settlement house where she worked, and she decided—no doubt urged by Putnam—to pursue a career as an aviator. Giving up social work was likely a painful decision for Earhart. Her work among immigrant families had been deeply gratifying, fulfilling twin desires to act on her progressive politics and to build an independent career. In the early part of the twentieth century, most professions were closed to women. Social work was one of the few fields dominated by women, including those who shared Earhart's progressive social views. Eleanor Roosevelt, later a close friend of Earhart's, had herself worked in a settlement house. In the years leading up to Earhart's arrival at Denison House, she had resisted the conventional path for women but was unsure of how to carve out a different one for herself. After stints as a volunteer nurse in Canada during World War I and a year at Columbia with the aim of becoming a doctor, Earhart followed her family to Los Angeles, largely to bolster her parents' failing marriage. It was in Los Angeles that Earhart began taking flying lessons with female aviator Neta Snook after being thrilled by a ride at a fair. To support the lessons, Earhart held down, by her own account, twenty-eight jobs during this period. Her stint as a truck driver for a gravel-hauling operation signals her unconventionality and willingness to cross gender boundaries from an early age; her time spent as an assistant to a portrait photographer may have contributed to her knack for presenting herself to the many cameras she would face in the coming years. After her parents' marriage finally dissolved, Earhart returned to Boston with her mother. Jobless, lacking in confidence and direction, she was still determined not to concede to her fiancé's requests that she marry and "settle down." In her student days, Earhart had kept a scrapbook of articles about women's professional accomplishments and, though nearing thirty, she was not ready to surrender her dream of joining their ranks. She was placed at Denison House by the Women's Educational and Industrial Union, where she quickly distinguished herself as a social worker. She would refer to herself as an aviator *and* social worker throughout her life, and often visited settlement houses in cities along her flight path. The establishment of an independent career, especially one that provided the social support and solidarity of other women the way Denison House did, was key to Earhart's sense of possibility and accomplishment, and to her ability to relate and appeal to other women as her fame grew.

Capitalizing on that fame was critical to further opportunities for flying. Immediately after the 1928 flight, Putnam—following the blueprint he had perfected for Lindbergh, who wrote the bestselling *We* after his solo Atlantic crossing—commissioned Earhart to write a book based on her in-flight account. *20 Hrs. 40 Min.* was in stores less than three months later. Sidonie Smith stresses the book's key role in shaping the personal narrative that laid the groundwork for Earhart's further celebrity. In addition to reinforcing and elaborating the biographical details that appeared in the press, the book was liberally illustrated with photographs. They were probably selected and sequenced by Putnam—even, in some cases, commissioned by him—and they reiterate the image of Earhart seen in newspapers and magazines. Smith describes them as framing devices that "package" Earhart as a particular kind of celebrity. Scholars of the Hollywood "star" system have argued that the celebrity figure "gives a form of embodiment to the mass subject," fleshing out for the consuming masses imaginary selves and imaginary lives through which they can fantasize future selves. For such an embodiment visibility is essential. Thus the obligatory photographs incorporated into the text. Identifying Earhart with the engine of modernity, the airplane, and with a monumental event, the flight across the Atlantic, the photos collectively present the spectacle of the exceptionalist individual—with a particular style of flesh. Free of fleshly excess, hers is a taut body designed functionally for mobility, a virtually weightless body that appears to have severed the relationship of femininity and sessility. Mannish, even boyish, the "slim, exercised, and active feminine body" of the aviatrix signifies, according to Barbara Green, "a pared-down modernism and machine-age aesthetic."[11]

In her close reading of the book, Smith also calls attention to its rarely used full title: *20 Hrs. 40 Min. Our Flight in the Friendship, the American Girl, First Across the Atlantic by Air, Tells Her Story*. Referring to Earhart as an "American Girl" casts her achievement in terms of national progress rather than gender transgression, and reinforced her femininity as youthful and innocent rather than sexualized. Additionally, her self-deprecating, antiheroic humor and insistence that she flew for "the fun of it" (the title of her next book) served to domesticate and normalize flight, making her less threatening and promoting the interests of the fledgling commercial aviation industry.

20 Hrs. 40 Min. was just one element of the promotional vehicle set up to take advantage of Earhart's popularity following the 1928 flight. Putnam helped arrange speaking engagements, endorsements, and a writing contract with *McCall's* magazine. There were occasional missteps: Earhart's advertisement for Lucky Strike, which used one of the "Lady Lindy" photographs, was considered "unladylike" by *McCall's*, and the magazine cancelled her contract. *Cosmopolitan* was untroubled by the endorsement, and offered Earhart the position of "aviation editor." Beginning in November 1928, she contributed articles to the magazine on a monthly basis for the next year, and periodically thereafter. The articles focused on her flight experiences and encouraged other women to embrace flying, and were usually accompanied by photographs of Earhart. The first and most striking of these articles includes pictures apparently taken by *Cosmopolitan* staff photographers[12] combined with well-circulated press images. A double-page spread of text and six photos, all equally sized, features two of the "Lady Lindy" images and four by a *Cosmopolitan* staff photographer, including images of Earhart in an elegant drop-waisted dress, in tennis uniform with racket, and in riding clothes—jodhpurs, shirt, and tie, crop in hand—complete with props. Including images of Earhart in athletic gear references the sports culture of the 1920s, and casts her flying as yet another sport for the affluent. The effect of so many different costumes on the same figure is rather like a book of paper dolls—in one sense, the idea that women are free to choose from a range of identities is liberating. At the same time, the notion that Earhart's identity as flyer is just another outfit that can be taken off and replaced with a dress or tennis gear undermines the seriousness of her commitment.[13]

Between 1928 and her next triumph in 1932, Earhart continued to fly but was not front-page news. Maintaining her popularity between flights was essential, since flying was a very costly pursuit and hard to fund, particularly after the stock market crash in 1929. In order to fly, she needed to raise money; in order to raise money, she needed to maintain her celebrity. She did this through writing, lecturing, endorsements (which both capitalized on and reproduced her celebrity), and events that served as photoops. A deep-sea dive in 1929 made the front page of *Mid-Week Pictorial*, a photo supplement of the *New York Times* and precursor to picture magazines such as *Life* and *Look*, which came out on Wednesdays and augmented the Sunday rotogravure section of the paper. Earhart, who was both newsworthy and visually appealing, was a staple of *Mid-Week Pictorial*, which relied heavily on photographs from the newspaper.[14] In addition to participating in events that would ensure press coverage, Earhart appeared in photographs with other celebrities, including members of the Hollywood elite, which underscored her own stardom and implied a life of glamour.

Most of these promotional efforts were spearheaded by Putnam, who by this time was acting as her manager. In 1931, he also became her husband. Earhart was deeply ambivalent about marriage and outlined her concerns in a letter to Putnam that served as a prenuptial agreement: "You must know again my reluctance to marry, my feeling that I shatter thereby chances in work which mean much to me. I feel the move just now as foolish as anything I could do. I know there may be compensations, but have no heart to look ahead." She concluded by dismissing the "medieval" idea of monogamy, and demanding that the two part ways after a year if the marriage did not seem to be working out. There was much speculation at the time and since about Putnam's role in her career. It is undeniable that his efforts on Earhart's behalf were essential to her celebrity, and therefore to her continued ability to fly. His connections at the *New York Times*, Paramount, and other media outlets gave her access that she would not otherwise have had. Publicists and image managers were key to the still relatively new operation of humaninterest journalism and celebrity that emerged in the early twentieth century. Putnam's untiring work on her behalf, however self-serving, was instrumental. But given the importance Earhart placed on independence and self-determination, it is hard to imagine that Putnam played a Svengali-like role in her life and career, though the inclination to look for the male author of female success was as prevalent then as it is now. A far more likely scenario is that she was a full and willing participant in his efforts, and that he should be understood as working for her rather than vice versa.

The May 1932 issue of *Vanity Fair* featured Earhart among a number of notable American women flyers in an article entitled "When Ladies Take the Air." Unbeknownst to the magazine, a few weeks later Earhart would make a flight that would definitively distinguish her from that crowded field. After three years spent honing her flying skills and refining her public persona, Earhart quietly began preparations for the first solo flight across the Atlantic by a woman. If successful, it would make her the first person (male or female) to accomplish such a feat since Lindbergh, further solidifying the connection in the public mind between her and her male counterpart. She had several rivals in this endeavor, including Ruth Nichols and Elinor Smith, both popular figures nearly as well known as Earhart, whose intentions were covered with excitement by the press. By contrast, Earhart kept her plans a closely guarded secret, and it was a great surprise when she launched from Harbor Grace, Newfoundland, on May 20, 1932, the fifth anniversary of Lindbergh's flight. She made the crossing successfully, despite an engine fire that caused her to land in Ireland rather than to retrace Lindbergh's flight and land in Paris. As in 1928, her laudatory reception in Europe was followed closely by the press, but this time she did not have to disavow or explain her role. The flight was Earhart's greatest triumph and launched her to greater levels of renown. It would silence critics who had dismissed her as little more than "a sack of potatoes" on the 1928 flight, and was also essential to her own need to prove herself. She later wrote, "I wanted to justify myself to myself. I wanted to prove that I deserved at least a small fraction of the nice things said about me." But, she continued, "there were other reasons—stronger than this . . . simply stated, that women can do most things that men can do."

This self-assurance is apparent in images promoting the flight, in which she is depicted either in a leather flying jumpsuit, as in a series of photographs in London, or simplified, elegant sportswear or eveningwear that emphasizes her slenderness and mobility. As her image is refined, stock poses and thematic tropes recur. A widely reproduced studio portrait of Earhart shows her in a velvet dress with a pearl necklace draped over her honorary major's flying wings pin. In this image, the signifier of her flying achievements is commingled with those of femininity and class status. A photograph of Earhart just before her 1928 flight in an open cockpit and flying helmet, holding a string of pearls between her fingers, was similarly adopted as an expedient image to convey the notion of aviatrix: a daring but genteel "lady flyer." Ware writes that the effect of combined male and female signifiers in the photos is "powerful, compelling, yet also destabilizing; especially in the context of 1930s gender roles."[15] This balancing of symbols within the image is not unlike layouts that feature a pairing of photographs of Earhart in and out of flying clothes.[16] Other posing conventions are also notable for their frequent occurrence. The image of a machine-savvy woman was still fascinating to the public, so many photographs show Earhart at the controls of her cockpit. Yet other images take this theme a step further and show Earhart's body melded in some way with the plane: holding her propeller, or with the ring of her radio direction finder playfully held up to frame her face. These motifs were refined and repeated in photographs widely reproduced in the press for nearly a decade, contributing to the vision of what women could do and look like.

The recognition Earhart garnered for her 1932 solo flight translated into further revenue from endorsements and public appearances. She wrote a second book, *The Fun of It*, completing all but the last chapter before making the flight. She endorsed a line of luggage that was carried by Macy's and even featured by the store in a large window display replicating a cockpit and including enlarged photographs of Earhart. An excerpt from *The Fun of It* was used as a double-page ad for Kodak, which ran in *House and Garden* in April 1933. Despite revenue from these ventures, neither Earhart nor Putnam were wealthy, so finding new ways to make her flying self-sustaining was an essential and constant search.

In 1935, when Earhart was named one of America's best-dressed women by Fashion Designers of America, the honor was based less on her flight clothes than the simple and tasteful evening gowns and well-tailored skirt suits in which she was often photographed, as well as the effortless elegance of her slender frame. The award may also have been a nod to Earhart's short-lived foray into clothing design the year before, when Earhart and Putnam determined that her distinctive and popular personal style could be the basis for a line of clothing for modern, active women. In addition to providing another source of revenue, the fashion line would also serve the function of underscoring Earhart's femininity. "A sense of design and color had never been her strong suit," writes Karla Jay, "but it seemed crucial to her image to show she was not a masculine impersonator: she was an all-around American girl. In fact, she was an archetypal superwoman. Not only was she the first woman to fly across the Atlantic alone, she thriftily patterned her own clothing at home . . ."[17] The styles of the Earhart line—which she most likely did not design herself, press photographs of her hard at work with a dressmaker notwithstanding—were pitched to the active modern woman but did not differ substantially from widely available mainstream fashions of 1934. Neither did they reference the more subversive aspects of Earhart's sartorial choices: nowhere among the garments were the ties, leather jackets, and jodhpurs that she wore when flying. Though Earhart worked hard to make the business that bore her name successful, the new venture was ill-timed, launched in the midst of the Depression. The average woman was unlikely to spend much of her meager resources keeping up with fashion trends; moreover, sewing patterns copying popular styles were widely available. A one-page spread in *Vogue* of June 1, 1934, features Earhart modeling two of her designs, unremarkable skirt-and-jacket ensembles. Photographed in relaxed but conventional poses by Anton Bruehl and Frederick Bradley, these images bear little trace of the fascination generated by photographs of Earhart the aviator. An August issue of *Woman's Home Companion* includes a photograph of Earhart, her lithe frame casually slouched in a chair and clothed in yet another tasteful but unexceptional suit. The accompanying copy claims that "We may not pilot a plane, we may not play opposite Tilden on the courts, but we do lead active lives, nearly all of us." Readers of the magazine, potential consumers of the line, are encouraged to see themselves in the Earhart mold; their own, modern lives are but slightly less spectacular versions of hers.

The clothing line folded after one season. But the substantial amount of time it took to promote it left Earhart exhausted and distracted from the business of flying. She and Putnam turned to more lucrative, but also more controversial, enterprises. The relationship between aviation and promotion or "ballyhoo" was a close one. Many of the early flyers, while on the one hand seen as exciting avatars of modernism, also faced charges of stunting, self-promotion, and theatricality. Even Lindbergh, who was vocally opposed to commercialization and lionized for his squeaky-clean image, faced criticism.[18] Despite the openly commercial nature of many of her promotional activities, Earhart was able to side-step scrutiny until late in her career, when two record-breaking flights were tainted with accusations of inappropriate commercialism. In 1935, she was the first person to fly solo from Hawaii to the mainland. In a January 30, 1935, editorial entitled "Sticky Business," *The Nation* wrote that "the recent thrilling flight of Amelia Earhart was merely the most spectacular of several projects in ballyhoo designed and paid for by the Pan-Pacific Press Bureau to increase the profits of Hawaiian sugar planters." While recognizing her courage and her genuine passion for aviation, the article nonetheless pointed out that Earhart was privately paid to promote the image of Hawaii as part of the United States. The Sugar Planters' Association, it was claimed, hoped to use Earhart's trip as part of a publicity campaign to lift sugar quotas imposed on territorial possessions. "Such transactions are generally regarded as corrupt, though her best friend—presumably her husband, who arranged the terms—neglected to tell her so." Later that year, she faced similar criticisms after another record-breaking flight to Mexico. "Under the management of her publicity-conscious husband," the flight coincided with an NBC radio campaign to promote tourism in Mexico, and Earhart also benefited financially from sales of commemorative stamps. Upon landing in Newark after the flight, Earhart defended herself with a pointed rejoinder: "I fly better than I wash dishes. I try to make my flying self-supporting. I could not fly otherwise."[19]

These isolated instances of criticism did not diminish public admiration for Earhart, which she was able to parlay into advocacy for issues dear to her. By the mid-1930s, her celebrity was secure enough that she could use her image to accomplish objectives other than its perpetuation. An avowed proponent of women's rights throughout her career, she supported passage of an Equal Rights Amendment, joining a National Women's Party delegation to the White House. She encouraged other female aviators and was a founding member of the Ninety-Nines, an association of women flyers. She also worked on behalf of the aviation industry, beginning with her representation of Kinner planes even before her launch to fame. In the 1920s and '30s, the industry was in the process of radical transition. No longer "an exciting but somewhat useless toy," the airplane was becoming a viable means of transportation, and air flight a potentially lucrative industry. But the public still associated flying with danger—not incorrectly, since the deaths of many early flyers were covered in the news. The common conception of the "intrepid birdman," the daring and athletic "modern superman" of the first decade of aviation, was anathema to an industry seeking to put the average person in a commercial plane. In the effort to domesticate the skies, women became essential. "Prejudice, paradoxically, begat opportunity" for women, writes aviation historian Joseph Corn.[20] Earhart and nearly all of the other big-name women flyers at some point in their careers found jobs demonstrating and selling planes, and aviation manufacturers willingly provided planes or other support to women's flying events in the interest of convincing the public that flying was safe and easy: as one female aviator said, if women can do it, "the public thinks it must be duck soup for men."[21] Women aviators seized the opportunities offered to them, despite the motive. Many of them believed strongly in the importance of aviation. But their dedication ultimately worked against them. Women like Earhart were asked to make their own achievements seem unremarkable in the service of an industry that shut them out entirely once they had served their purpose.

In 1936, Earhart accepted a position as consultant to the newly formed department of the study of careers for women at Purdue University in Indiana. She was able to pursue her passion for teaching young women and encouraging their careers, while also finding a new—and perhaps more respectable—way to support her flying. The president of Purdue announced a fund for aviation research which would supply Earhart with a plane for one last record-breaking flight. Calling her new Lockheed Electra the "flying laboratory," Earhart tried to circumvent critics who might claim that her aim was to keep her name in the papers. Instead, the "flying laboratory" was positioned to study a range of effects of flying on humans, and thereby contribute meaningful data to the industry. The announced route was a circumnavigation of the globe at the equator. Such a flight, which would have been a source of fascination and celebration in previous years, was described as "back-page news" by *Time* magazine: the era of aviation heroics had come to an end, and a flight of this sort was becoming an anachronism. With the advent of commercial aviation, the figure of the hero-aviator was replaced by the (male) career pilot. After peaking in 1932 and remaining steady through 1935, Earhart's popularity was beginning to wane.

Photographs of Earhart before the 1937 flight follow many of the posing conventions that had been established with previous flights: she is shown at the controls of her plane, demonstrating that the image of a woman mastering complex machinery was still a source of fascination for viewers. Images of Earhart and Putnam make visual play of their inverted gender roles: she studies an unrolled map while he looks on; she stands on the wing of her plane to bid him farewell, recalling a comment in *Literary Digest* before her transatlantic flight in 1932: "We are all used to the picture of the adventurer's wife sitting at home waiting for his safe return. But to see the husband in such a role is not so common."

Though the flight did not garner the attention of earlier record-breaking ones, a number of photographs exist from various stops along the route, in South America, Africa, and Southeast Asia. Earhart herself took photographs along the way, and sent them back to her husband. One of the last photographs to be taken is a casual image of Earhart and her navigator, Fred Noonan, in Bandung, Indonesia. The image was sent by radio—wire photos had come into general use the year before—from London to New York, and was widely distributed and described in the press as the last photo taken of the pair. (In fact, photographs were taken in the following days in Lae, though they were not circulated in the press.)

After more than five weeks of flying, on July 2, 1937, Earhart and Noonan took off for Howland, a tiny island in the South Pacific with a single airstrip built specifically for Earhart with WPA funds. This was to be the final leg of the journey before departing for Hawaii. Hours passed and the plane failed to appear at Howland; radio communication was unsuccessful. Reports of the U.S. Navy's extensive sea and air search appeared on the front page of every American newspaper for days. In the absence of photographic evidence of a crash, papers ran a combination of stock portraits of the pair, maps of the planned route, and even drawings of Earhart and Noonan adrift on their plane in shark-infested waters. As the chances for rescue dimmed, newspapers and magazines began to run tributes to Earhart, in place of obituaries. *Life* magazine published a three-page photo-story on the flight; surprisingly, it was the first article on Earhart to run in the picture magazine, founded a year before; a photo of children playing in the spray of a fire hydrant, not Earhart, made the cover. Entitled "Log of Earhart's 'Last Stunt Flight,'"[22] the layout features an image that was reproduced repeatedly in coverage of the disappearance. Taken when she disclosed plans for the flight, it shows her response to a reporter who asked how big Howland would look on a map compared to the other places she would visit. Laughing, Earhart holds up her hand to indicate the miniscule size of the island. The image could be read as confirmation of her dare-devil nature: she was aware of the risks she faced, and took up the challenge with spirit and style. Just as easily, the popularity of the image among photo editors—along with a faintly ridiculous photo of Earhart in a rubber escape raft from her Hawaii trip—betray an undercurrent of disapproval or even derision that is also to be found in textual accounts of the disappearance. The implication in these stories is that her desire to prove herself, and other women, caused her to get in over her head. In what was supposed to be an editorial tribute to Earhart, *Aviation* magazine lets loose a finger-wagging rebuke: though she "combined native capacity for quick decision and direct action with feminine charm and personality . . . her greatest weakness was her extreme consciousness that she was a woman. Obvious in all her activities, since she rode as 'a sack of ballast' across the Atlantic in the Friendship in 1928, was the constant drive to undertake difficult things just to prove that she (as a woman) could do them. It is not difficult to see that such an urge might sooner or later get her into trouble. . . . At most it [her last flight] would have contributed little or nothing to the knowledge of commercial ocean flying that is now the most important field for the future. The real tragedy of Amelia Earhart is that hers was the psychology of the Age of the Vikings applied at a time when aviation had already passed over into the Age of the Clipper."[23]

Despite uncharitable displays of *schadenfreude* by a few critics, Earhart's loss caused a national outpouring of grief, and her contributions to aviation and her significance as an inspiration were remembered. In response to renewed interest in his wife, Putnam embellished and published *Last Flight*, Earhart's unfinished chronicle. He followed up the next year with *Soaring Wings*, a biographical portrait that met with modest success. Her dramatic end did not produce an immediate apotheosis. As Europe and then the United States headed into war, Earhart and her disappearance receded from the public eye.[24] It was not until anti-Japanese sentiment fomented by the war led to speculation that Earhart wound up a Japanese prisoner of war that her image returned to the popular consciousness. A 1943 movie starring Rosalind Russell and Fred MacMurray, *Flight from Freedom*, promoted the idea that Earhart and Noonan were on a spy mission for the government when captured by the Japanese. A 1946 letter to the editor in *Time* magazine ran a photo of Earhart in Southeast Asia that was claimed to have been "taken from a dead Jap"—further evidence of Japanese involvement. In fact, the photograph was reproduced in *Last Flight* and would have been widely available. Conspiracy theories about Earhart's disappearance often employed photographs of the aviator, ensuring that her image would remain identifiable to subsequent generations. These photographs were used as proof of a range of theories. To support his 1970 book *Amelia Earhart Lives*, which claims that Earhart was alive and living in New Jersey and had been captured by the Japanese and forced to broadcast to American soldiers as Tokyo Rose, Joe Klaas reproduced a photograph of Earhart in a kimono, participating in a Japanese tea service. Distributed through UPI as publicity for Klaas's book, the photograph was actually taken during Earhart's 1935 visit to Hawaii.

In addition to the unending stream of disappearance theories, Earhart's image was given new life by the women's movement of the 1970s. Recuperated as a feminist icon, Earhart was referenced in Judy Chicago's monument to women's achievement, *The Dinner Party* (1974–79), and featured on the cover of a 1976 issue of *Ms.*—complete with t-shirt iron-on. *The Fun of It* was reissued in 1977; an image of Earhart in pearls and flying cap graces the front cover, while the back features a quote as relevant to the 1970s as it was to the '30s: "Women must try to do things as men have tried. When they fail, their failure must be but a challenge to others." And the plethora of illustrated biographies aimed at children published since her disappearance indicate that she remained a figure deemed an appropriate model for young people, particularly girls. Earhart's message resonated across generations, and her image continued to be the bearer of the ideals she embodied.

Newspapers, magazines, newsreels, and books from Earhart's lifetime demonstrate that her image was surprisingly varied for a public figure. To her contemporaries, she was identifiable in eveningwear at a White House function, a skirt suit giving a lecture on women in aviation, or in a leather flying jacket and pants. Indeed, her continued popularity was probably dependent upon a carefully calibrated balance of these images. Too masculine and she would have been seen as threatening; too feminine and she would lose the source of difference that made her image fascinating. Though the image of Earhart commanding technology and dressing in a way that signaled physical and social freedom was often presented in ways that constrained or modified that freedom, it was nonetheless a powerful symbol, particularly to women.

As time passes, Earhart is revered less for what she did than what she stands for. Correspondingly, her iconic photographic image today is much more singular than it was in her own time, when a public very familiar with her narrative could identify and was interested in images of her in a range of activities and guises. She has become an increasingly abstract symbol—of the thrill and danger of adventure, of the possibilities for women, and of the courage to break with the past and conventional expectations. In this process, her image has become consolidated, and only those photographs that convey those ideals can stand in for her. A dramatic and conspiracy theory–plagued disappearance (rather than death) has kept her narrative open-ended, and aided in the afterlife of photographs of Earhart. But it is the continued need for a symbol of the ideals she embodies that is the source of their relevance and appeal.

Notes

1 A similar photo from the same period shows Earhart in tie, leather jacket, and pants, hand resting lightly on the wheel of the Vega. This image was not, it seems, reproduced widely—if at all—at the time, and would have been an unlikely choice for an advertiser today. Though remarkably similar to the Gap image, the portrait bears a surfeit of masculine signifiers; instead of the softly tied scarf in the Gap photo, she wears a tie. Instead of an unthreatening pose with hands stuffed in pockets, she faces the camera self-assuredly and physically declares her connection with her machine. In contrast, in both the Gap and Apple ads, the insinuation of gender play pushes the envelope of conventionality just enough to create intrigue without going so far as to be destabilizing or off-putting to potential customers.

2 This can be seen in several photographs of Earhart from the years leading up to her 1928 flight, including the oft-reproduced photograph from her first pilot's license.

3 Doris L. Rich, *Amelia Earhart: A Biography* (Washington, DC: Smithsonian Institution Press, 1989), p. 32, quoted in Susan Ware, *Still Missing: Amelia Earhart and the Search for Modern Feminism* (New York: W. W. Norton, 1993), p. 145.

4 Hilton H. Railey, *Touch'd with Madness* (New York: Carrick and Evans, 1938), p. 100.

5 Quoted in Anne Herrmann, "Amelia Earhart: The Aviatrix as American Dandy," in *Queering the Moderns* (New York: Palgrave, 2000), p. 21.

6 Quoted in Susan Butler, *East to the Dawn: The Life of Amelia Earhart* (New York: Da Capo Press, 1999), p. 168.

7 Ware, *Still Missing*, p. 21.

8 Charles L. Ponce de Leon, "The Man Nobody Knows: Charles Lindbergh and the Culture of Celebrity," *Prospects* 21 (1996), p. 356.

9 Estelle B. Freedman discusses 1930s characterizations of women of the '20s, which focused on moral and social aspects rather than women's political or economic concerns: "women in the 1920s began to be presented as flappers, more concerned with clothing and sex than with politics. Women had by choice, the accounts suggested, rejected political emancipation and found sexual freedom. The term feminism nearly disappeared from historical accounts, except in somewhat pejorative references to the Woman's party." See "The New Woman: Changing Views of Women in the 1920s," *Journal of American History* 61 (September 1974), p. 379.

10 Herrmann, "Amelia Earhart: The Aviatrix as American Dandy," p. 27.

11 Sidonie Smith, "Virtually Modern Amelia: Mobility, Flight, and the Discontents of Identity," in *Virtual Gender: Fantasies of Subjectivity and Embodiment*, edited by Mary Ann O'Farrell and Lynne Vallone (Ann Arbor: University of Michigan Press, 1999), p. 26.

12 All of these photographs appear to have been lost during the disposal of the Hearst Archive.

13 A 1987 book of "famous American women" paper dolls echoes this idea. Earhart "at a press conference," in skirt and heels, is the doll, whereas the "flying attire"—pants, leather jacket, and oxfords—is the costume to put over the doll. (Gertrude Stein's doll does Earhart one better: Alice B. Toklas is part of the "costume" she can wear.)

14 Though very often in newspapers, she was less likely to be found pictured in the pages of illustrated magazines, and, with one exception (*McCall's*), never on their covers.

15 Ware, *Still Missing*, p. 169.

16 It is difficult to ascribe authorship to these conventions. Because archives do not exist that describe in detail the promotional materials that Putnam distributed to the press, we cannot determine the degree of control that he asserted over which photographs were distributed, used, and how they were captioned or positioned. The majority of the photographs of Earhart that appeared in print were taken by news photographers at public events, not by studio photographers under the pay and direction of Earhart or Putnam.

17 Karla Jay, "No Bumps, No Excrescences: Amelia Earhart's Failed Flight into Fashions," in *On Fashion*, edited by Shari Benstock and Suzanne Ferriss (New Brunswick, NJ: Rutgers University Press, 1994), p. 86.

18 Lindbergh, who was so popular as to be untouchable by the press, was finally and resoundingly criticized in a two-part article in *The New Yorker* (September 20 and 27, 1930), which alleged that his decline of offers of commercial profit was in the interest of gleaning larger profits from the aviation industry, and that he was a pawn of the business. "He was shrewd enough to see that if he harkened to the ballyhoo, limbo lay close ahead and the career was impossible." Instead, he plucked "the few rich plums that he could take without the charge of greediness from the enormous harvest proffered him by fame." The article concludes by deeming Lindbergh "a public performer" who has contributed little to the serious advance of aviation: "He has simply done a lot of excellent stunt flying."

19 *News-week*, May 18, 1935, pp. 34–35.

20 Joseph J. Corn, "Making Flying 'Thinkable': Women Pilots and the Selling of Aviation, 1927–1940," *American Quarterly* 31, no. 4 (1979), p. 560.

21 Ibid., p. 559.

22 *Life*, July 19, 1937, pp. 21–23. Following the brief tribute to Earhart's "last stunt flight" is a spread labeled "non-stunt flight," about transatlantic survey flights by Pan American and Imperial Airways, "pure commercial flying, the finest of its kind in the world" (p. 24).

23 *Aviation* (August 1937). This criticism could be seen as an extension of what Freedman terms "the Depression psychology which sought to bring women out of the work force. While legal and political equality were praised, social and cultural emancipation evoked gentle reproaches." Freedman, "The New Woman," p. 383.

24 Susan Ware describes Earhart's post-disappearance fade from notoriety and subsequent resurgence in detail in *Still Missing*, pp. 224–26.

THIRTY-NINE FOREVER

Susan Butler

Good looks, good judgment, good temperament, a will to win, a sense of mission, a taste for adventure, a born leader who wanted to leave the world a better place than she found it—those words describe Amelia Earhart.

The breadth of her interests and the deftness with which she drew attention to her enterprises was astounding. She relished the platform fame gave her and exploited it to push her agenda: that women should be educated and independent, that women should control their own lives, that women should be all that they could be. In an age when discrimination made a career in law, medicine, engineering, or business a rarity for women, she was a voice for change. Consciously, she held herself out as the attainable future of womanhood and her life as an attainable lifestyle that young women could and should strive for. She had achieved the impossible twin peaks—a glamorous, devoted husband and a glorious career, and she was constantly reminding women that they, too, could have both.

Her aviation record was astounding. She was easily the most famous, most distinguished aviatrix of her day.

She was born in Atchison, Kansas, in 1897, and raised there by her grandparents, Alfred and Amelia Otis, both of whose forebears had been in America for generations. Alfred, a young lawyer, one of the first settlers in the newly platted town of Atchison, was an abolitionist who put down roots there in time to cast his vote in 1857 for Kansas to enter the Union a free rather than slave state. He became an extremely successful lawyer. He and his wife Amelia, after whom Earhart was named, prospered and with the passage of years became surrounded by family and friends with ties to most of the people of consequence in the state. Their daughter Amy married Edwin Earhart, the son of a Lutheran minister whose family, of German background, had also been in America since before the Revolution. While Amy and Edwin made their home in Kansas City, they allowed the Otises to raise Amelia and send her to the private school in Atchison where Amy had gone as a child. The experience made Amelia unshakably independent.

A life of the mind, combined with a life of purpose and action, was how Amelia as a young woman described the future she envisioned for herself. On vacation in Toronto, while a student at Ogontz, a finishing school outside of Philadelphia, she had been so stunned at the sight of the many Canadian soldiers who had lost arms and legs fighting in World War I that she never returned to school, instead becoming a nurse's aid at the Spadina Military Hospital in Toronto. There she cared for the injured, then, as the war wound down, ministered to the soldiers stricken by the flu pandemic. She ended up working the night shift in the pneumonia ward, until she, too, was stricken. After a long convalescence, Amelia enrolled at Columbia University with the intention of becoming a doctor, but after a year, heeding the entreaties of her parents, who had settled in Los Angeles, she reluctantly went west to live with them.

There, in 1921, before the invention of parachutes, when planes still dropped out of the sky as their engines quit, she fell in love with flying. Within a short time, she had established a new altitude record for women, and in 1923 was the first of her sex to be granted an FAI license by the National Aeronautic Association. She flew in the Aerial Rodeos which were such popular events in California in those years, and became a local celebrity as mention of her with the glamorous Hollywood movie stars with whom she flew appeared in the newspapers. The plane she bought, a Kinner Airster, and her testimonial as to its sterling qualities appeared as advertisements in flying magazines. But Amelia, still in her twenties, had been living with her parents, whose marriage was breaking up, and there was no money to spare. She needed a serious profession. She thought of flying as a sport, as did everyone else, and in the 1920s sports did not pay. So she again enrolled at Columbia, but her newly divorced parents could not support years of medical education and she was forced to quit. Moving to Boston, where her mother had taken a house, she looked for work.

Earhart became a social worker at Denison House, which had been founded by three female Wellesley professors. In those years, social work was that rare profession in which a woman could rise to power and prominence. Eleanor Roosevelt was a social worker, as was Frances Perkins, whom Franklin Roosevelt appointed secretary of labor. Jane Addams, the famous founder of Hull House, was the first woman to earn an honorary degree from Yale. Within a short time, Earhart was on the Denison House board of directors; within two years, she was representing it at national settlement house conferences.

But flying was in her blood, and it was as a flyer that Boston first heard of her. She found time to become affiliated with and to fly out of a new airport near the city; she joined the local chapter of the National Aeronautic Association, whose members, quickly recognizing her ability and charm, nominated her to be their first female vice-president. She hit the local newspapers when she flew over Boston scattering leaflets to advertise a fundraising affair at Denison House. She wrote an article for *The Bostonian*, the magazine all Boston read, called "When Women Go Aloft," which appeared in the May 1928 issue. When a well-known German aviatrix, Thea Rasche, crash-landed during an air exhibition, Earhart took to the skies in a Waco 10 and gave what the newspapers called "an excellent demonstration of flying." She did it, she told the waiting reporter, because she "wanted to prove that Miss Rasche's mishap was unavoidable and no fault of her own; that women are quite as capable pilots as men, and quite as daring."

Earhart always took care to project an image of personal competence. A few years before, when she and another female pilot had crash-landed in Los Angeles, worried that lurking reporters might write of finding flustered, nervous, demoralized aviatrixes, immediately after cutting the power switch she began powdering her nose. "We have to look nice when the reporters come," she said to her amazed co-pilot. Her statement to the waiting reporter was the first time she consciously used her notoriety to emphasize female competence. It can be argued that it was her background in social work that gave Amelia the standing, the moral authority, to speak up for women.

She leapt to international fame in 1928 when she became the first woman to fly across the Atlantic. Even though she was only a passenger, the flight was a major first because it was considered to be such a daring feat. Following Lindbergh's epic flight, five adventurous women had attempted to be the first woman, each of them taking a man aboard to help fly the plane. They included an English princess, a Viennese actress, an American beauty-contest winner, a niece of Woodrow Wilson, and England's most glamorous aviatrix, the Honorable Elsie Mackay, raven-haired daughter of Lord Inchcape. The Viennese actress was the luckiest—her plane never became airborne. The beauty contest winner was rescued at sea. The other three—the princess, Wilson's niece, and Mackay, all pilots themselves—went to their deaths somewhere in the North Atlantic.

The wealthy, well-connnected American Amy Phipps Guest, big-game hunter, crack rider, entrepreneur, mother of three grown children, wife of the former British air secretary Frederick Guest, decided the honor should be hers: she would beat out the rest of her sex and become the most famous woman in the world. She hired Richard E. Byrd to superintend the enterprise. Byrd bought her a three-engine Fokker, hired two top pilots, and set about working out the many details involved in the undertaking. Then Guest's family (her children mainly) talked her out of the trip. She relented on the condition that a proper substitute be found, stipulating that her replacement must be an educated American woman, of pleasing appearance, a pilot if possible, "Someone nice who will do us proud." So a search began.

The publisher George Palmer Putnam became involved in the search. Putnam's fascination with adventuring and heroes had led him to publish virtually every book written in the genre (and in some cases help shape the expedition), including books by Charles Lindbergh, Richard E. Byrd, Lincoln Ellsworth, General Billy Mitchell, William Beebe, and Roy Chapman Andrews. Because the Fokker was being fitted out in Boston, Boston was the first place inquiries were made to find a suitable woman; because Amelia was Boston's most famous aviatrix, she was the first woman interviewed. Her account of the meeting: ". . . if I were found wanting on too many counts I should be deprived of the trip. On the other hand, if I were just too fascinating the gallant gentlemen might be loath to drown me. Anyone can see the meeting was a crisis." Her fears notwithstanding, they loved her and chose her. No one else was interviewed.

The flight itself, in June of 1928, was a very close thing. Amelia and her two pilots were flying the Atlantic in a seaplane. This had been decided by Byrd, who had almost lost his life the year before when his landplane crash-landed in the surf off the French coast. He chose the harbor at Trepassey, Newfoundland, as the jumping-off place for the *Friendship* even though it was one of the foggiest venues in the world. Hindered by the weather and various mechanical problems, Earhart and her pilots were almost beaten out by another plane carrying another woman which was not only faster but looked like it would take off first. At the last moment, forced, as watching reporters could see, by Earhart, head pilot Wilmer Stultz reluctantly gathered the necessary supplies and he, his co-pilot, and Amelia took off in the *Friendship* into uncertain weather, heading east across the Atlantic. Twenty hours forty minutes later, having weathered storms, a general lack of visibility, and a nonworking radio, they landed in Burry Port, Wales, the Fokker's three engines sputtering as they drained the last drops of gas.

Earhart wrote up most of the account of the flight immediately, so that by the time she arrived in London it was running simultaneously in the *New York Times* and the *London Times* under her byline, as arranged by George Palmer Putnam.

The world went wild. For the rest of her life, Earhart was an international celebrity. Putnam published her story of the flight in a book released that fall, and, realizing that fame made her position as social worker at Denison House impossible, Earhart did not return to Boston. Instead, she moved to New York City and became the first aviation editor of *Cosmopolitan* magazine. Initially she lived at Greenwich House, a settlement house in the Village run by the renowned Mary Simkhovitch, and was a quasi-member of the staff. In 1929, she moved into the American Woman's Association, a new women's club/hotel, where she lived until her marriage to George Palmer Putnam in 1931.

Earhart's life fell into a pattern of record-breaking flights and lecturing to support the record-breaking flights. As the years went by and her fame grew, she carefully polished her image. The figure that has come down to us is of the androgynous flyer clad in shirt, pants, silk scarf, leather jacket, and goggles. The attractive casualness of Earhart's appearance was the result of attention to detail: her signature pants were of the best quality (she favored pants as much because they hid her one bad feature—thick ankles—as because they were more suited to flying), and she curled her hair to achieve a windblown look (even in remote Newfoundland she still curled her hair). Five foot eight, 118 pounds: she photographed well. But her contemporaries knew Amelia more than as a daring aviatrix. They saw the chic, contemplative woman that Steichen caught for *Vanity Fair*; they knew her as an intelligent lecturer and a committed educator.

On the lecture podium, she often wore dresses. Taking her cue from the way *Cosmopolitan* had presented her in photos in the fall of 1928—coiffed, sometimes draped in fur, casually feminine—especially when speaking to a mixed audience of men and women, she always appeared, in a word, *fashionable*. It pleased her and enhanced her message. To that mixed audience, her message was of the ease of flying, the worlds it opened up, the excitement, all of which she delivered in an engaging manner. To women's groups she spoke of those things also, but added thoughts on the importance of education and careers for women.

In the years following Lindbergh's flight, other flyers attempted to solo the North Atlantic, but none succeeded: two paid with their lives. Earhart's most daring achievement was that five years to the day after Lindbergh's flight she took off from Harbor Grace, Newfoundland, and, after a harrowing flight replete with equipment malfunctions and bad weather, safely landed her red single-engine Lockheed Vega in a farmer's field in Londonderry, Ireland.

The world was delirious. After the flight, according to Gore Vidal, who as a young boy knew her well, Earhart was elevated to almost mythic status. "Forget Garbo, forget Jackie, she was in a realm beyond stardom," he wrote.

Earhart set many flying records. She was not only the first woman to solo the North Atlantic, and the only flyer besides Lindbergh to accomplish that feat, the flight made her the first person to fly the Atlantic twice. She set women's speed records in 1930, was the first woman to accomplish a nonstop flight across the United States, and was the first woman to compete in and finish the Bendix race across the United States, the Kentucky Derby of the air world. She set an altitude record for autogiros of 18,451 feet that stood for years. She was the first pilot to fly solo from Honolulu to California, and the first pilot to fly solo nonstop from Mexico City to Newark.

Earhart's marriage was of a piece with the rest of her life: a demonstration of independence. The morning of the wedding, she handed Putnam a letter outlining her view of married life to make sure he did not expect her to be an ordinary bride. She demanded the right to be unfaithful and the right to leave him. ". . . I shall not hold you to any medieval code of faithfulness to me, nor shall I consider myself bound to you similarly. . . . let us not interfere with the other's work or play. . . . I must exact a cruel promise, and that is you will let me go in a year if we find no happiness together . . ."

Putnam, who adored her, not only signed on, from then on he devoted himself to promoting and facilitating her career. He did this even though he was fully aware of another man in her life. (After all, she had warned him.) *Time* magazine profiled Putnam as a person with a dangerous combination of literary ability, business acumen, and energy. He was also tall and good-looking, his glasses giving him more than a passing resemblance to Clark Kent. But Eugene Vidal was also devastatingly attractive. Gene was special. He had looks, intelligence, and incredible athletic ability. At West Point, he had been captain of the football team as well as the star of the basketball team; later he was a member of the 1920 U.S. Olympic team, placing in two of the three events he entered. And he was a flyer, West Point's first flying instructor. Earhart met him when they were both working for one of the first commercial airlines and they began an affair. She managed to keep everything very civilized; Gene and his son Gore often visited her in Rye, New York. Amelia and Gene were joined in a business venture, as two of the four incorporators of National Airways, which eventually became Northeast Airlines.

"A life of the mind, a life of purpose and action," as Earhart had articulated it as a young woman, became a description of her life. In 1929, she cofounded the Ninety-Nines, the first and still the most important women's flying organization, naming it for the number of women who signed up, thus avoiding all sorts of cutesy titles then being proposed. She was its first president and always one of its guiding lights. Whenever women pilots had a problem, they turned to her as spokesperson. Franklin and Eleanor Roosevelt both enjoyed her company and had her to stay at the White House. She was in demand as a lecturer all over the United States. In 1935, she spoke to 136 groups. In 1936, as she traveled the country, she campaigned for the president. At the Democratic Convention that year, she seconded the nomination of Caroline O'Day, a former neighbor in Rye, for a second congressional term; O'Day, New York's only female representative, won the race. Earhart testified on a variety of aviation issues before congressional committees. She was instrumental in convincing Roosevelt to appoint Eugene Vidal, respected as the brains behind one of the first successful commercial airlines, to the top civil job in aviation, director of the Bureau of Air Commerce.

Edward Elliott, president of Purdue University, heard Earhart speak at a conference and signed her on to the Purdue staff as lecturer on careers for women. It was his view that the effective employment of women was essential to the health and future of the United States. He planned to create a department for the study of careers for women with Earhart as the centerpiece, which would require her presence on campus for two weeks a semester. She immediately accepted. She was hugely popular with the girls, coeds, as they were called. The year after her appointment, coed applications jumped. One of her speeches ended, "If we begin to think and respond as capable human beings able to deal with and even enjoy the challenges of life, then we surely will have something more to contribute to marriage than our bodies." The engineering professors despised her, particularly as young women, influenced by Earhart's challenge, instead of signing up for home economics, began registering for engineering classes. Earhart wanted a new plane, and the Purdue Research Foundation agreed to buy her one with the understanding that the proceeds of any resultant research and book projects would revert to the university. Thus freed from financial constraints, she chose the twin-engine Lockheed Electra, a favorite of the airlines because it was the first fully pressurized plane and had a range of 4,000 miles. The only other individual who owned an Electra was the multimillionaire Howard Hughes.

Earhart planned to use the Lockheed to fly around the world at its waistline: the equator. It had never been done before. After that, she intended to hang up her adventuring spurs. She thought of it as her last record flight. It was planned to start and end in Hawaii, flying east to west. But the flight began badly: on take-off, the big plane groundlooped, damaging the wing and fuselage. By the time the Electra was repaired, weather patterns had changed, and a west-to-east route made more sense.

Earhart and her navigator, Fred Noonan, after a shakedown flight east across the United States, took off from Miami on June 1, 1937. They flew down the northeastern coast of South America, then straight across Central Africa, landing at Gao, Fort-Lamy, El Fasher, Khartoum, Massawa, Assab, then on to Karachi, Calcutta, Akyab, Rangoon, Bangkok, Singapore, Bandung, Surabaja, Kupang, Port Darwin, and Lae, New Guinea. As a child in Atchison, Amelia had invented a game called Bogey, which involved herself, her friends, and cousins piling into the abandoned carriage in her grandparents' barn which she would declare had turned into a magic chariot. Off they would go: the carriage would carry them to exotic, faraway, even dangerous places. Now she was living "those imaginary journeys full of fabulous perils," as she wrote in one of her last dispatches. She was living out her fantasy.

The riskiest part of the journey was the last stretch, the flight over the Pacific, from Lae, New Guinea, to tiny Howland Island, a mile and a half long by half a mile wide, where the Electra had to land to take on the fuel stashed there for the final leg to Hawaii. On the aborted trip from Hawaii, Earhart had had two navigators aboard to help her locate Howland. Now she had only one. Moreover, from Hawaii, Howland was only 1,800 miles; from Lae, it was 2,556 miles.

Earhart and Noonan took off from Lae and set a course east, expecting to reach Howland at dawn the next day. For whatever reason, whether they went too far or not far enough (no one is sure), they never found the island. The Coast Guard cutter *Itasca*, stationed at Howland to help guide Amelia in, had been transmitting weather reports to her and sending up plumes of black smoke as a visual aid. They intermittently heard her, and waited for the plane to appear. And waited. The world waited. They had disappeared.

No scrap of the Electra, no clue has ever been found. Although it was and still is the common assumption that they ran out of fuel, crash-landed in the sea, and sank, theories abound. People have spent years and fortunes trying to find the plane. For a long time, there were persistent rumors that Earhart and Noonan had been captured and tortured by the Japanese. The publicized rumors of Japanese mistreatment of Earhart suggested to the Japanese that Howland had strategic importance, possibly containing underground storage facilities. As a result, the day after Pearl Harbor, four Japanese planes attacked the island, followed by submarines that shelled it flat.

Earhart remains an icon, revered by young women, remembered by many for her signal accomplishments, remembered by all because of her dramatic end. She is thirty-nine forever.

It's Hard Work Being a Popular Heroine

Susan Ware

On August 6, 1926, a nineteen-year-old girl from New York named Gertrude Ederle became the first woman to swim the English Channel, besting by two hours the marks of the five men who had previously made the crossing. "I just knew if it could be done, it had to be done, and I did it," she told one of the swarm of reporters covering the attempt. On October 11, 1927, Ruth Elder took off for Paris in a bright orange single-engine Stinson aircraft called *The American Girl* with her flying instructor, George Haldeman, at the controls. After thirty-six hours in the air, an oil leak forced them down near the Azores, where they were dramatically rescued from the ocean just before their plane exploded and caught fire. On June 18, 1928, Amelia Earhart became the first woman to cross the Atlantic by plane and was subjected to the same media madness that had greeted Ederle and Elder. In fact, so interchangeable did these three popular heroines seem to the public that Amelia Earhart was twice congratulated for swimming the English Channel and often asked, "Weren't you lucky to be picked up by the steamer? Near the Azores, wasn't it?" As she put it slyly, "Elder, Ederle, Earhart—how thoughtless for all of us to have names that begin with E."[1]

What characterized a popular heroine in America in the 1920s and 1930s? She shared many characteristics with male heroes, such as Charles Lindbergh, Babe Ruth, Richard Byrd, Jack Dempsey, and Will Rogers. At first the recipient of spontaneous homage and acclaim for an act of individual achievement, she soon found herself the object of curiosity, identification, and imitation from fans and followers. Her admiring public honored the heroine's accomplishments through song, poems, and other accolades, grasped for tidbits about the heroine's life and values, and tried to establish personal relationships with its heroine through souvenir hunting, autograph collecting, and perhaps even a fleeting glimpse of the celebrity at a public function. Like heroes, heroines offered "inspiration . . . for rise in status" and served as "common symbols for identification . . . with whom the group feels a special pride and unity."[2] Amelia Earhart fitted this definition of hero worship exactly.

Because popular heroes and heroines usually burst on the scene with a dramatic feat of individual courage, they often appear curiously disconnected from their ensuing fame and adulation. Each was simply the right person in the right place at the right time. Perhaps this is what happened to Charles Lindbergh, but for all the rest, male and female, celebrity was not handed to them on a silver platter, and many found it difficult to capitalize on and sustain their initial success.[3]

Amelia Earhart's career confirms that there was no easy route to being a popular heroine. She had to make it happen, working on it practically every day of her life after her June 1928 flight had thrust her into the limelight. George Palmer Putnam, her husband and manager, captured this when he drew attention to "the sheer, thumping hard work of conscientious heroing."[4] For Earhart, it meant fourteen-hour days of lecturing and receptions, answering hundreds of letters a week from fans, cranking out instant books, dealing with newsreel photographers and reporters the very moment a grueling flight finished so they could make their deadlines, and always being on display wherever she went. By dint of hard work, skill, and luck, she was able to make a viable living out of promoting herself as an aviation celebrity. "I'm really very fortunate," she admitted, "because flying is both my business and my pleasure. I've got a job I love."[5]

But her "job" had a price. Just as Amelia had quipped in the 1920s, "No pay, no fly and no work, no play," she was caught in a similar cycle in which public appearances and endorsements were all part of what was necessary to earn money to allow her to fly. *Newsweek* captured the facts of life perfectly: "Every so often Miss Earhart, like other prominent flyers, pulls a spectacular stunt to hit the front pages. This enhances a flyer's value as a cigarette endorser, helps finance new planes, sometimes publicizes a book." She told an old flying friend in 1933: "It's a routine now. I make a record and then I lecture on it. That's where the money comes from. Until it's time to make another record." She did two major flights in 1935, candidly admitting after Mexico, "I expect to make quite a sum lecturing and writing for magazines about the trip."[6] In the end, she sustained public interest in her activities for close to a decade, quite a record of longevity for an American public notoriously fickle about its heroes and heroines.

It is hard to come to any assessment of Amelia Earhart's career without dealing with the overwhelming, if not overbearing, presence of George Palmer Putnam, who first entered her life as a manager in 1928 and added the role of husband in 1931. Aviator Bobbi Trout observed with more than a bit of asperity, "If I had a promoter like Putnam, I could have done the things Amelia did." One recent biographer went so far as to conclude that it was "mainly due to Putnam's brilliant management of the name Amelia Earhart that she is still remembered." The contrast between the well-liked, modest, and gracious Amelia Earhart and the opinionated, domineering, and aggressive George Palmer Putnam confused many who came into contact with them. But after all, she married him and was a willing, if not always eager, participant in his schemes and promotions. Fellow aviator Elinor Smith emphasized Earhart's active participation in the creation of her own career: "The image of a shy and retiring individual thrust against her will into the public eye was a figment of Putnam's lively imagination. Amelia was about as shy as Muhammad Ali."[7]

From 1928 on, Putnam had worked tirelessly and successfully to make the name Amelia Earhart synonymous with "best woman pilot" in the public mind, but his relentless publicizing did not always win him friends. There are legions of stories of his insensitivity if anyone got in the way of his promoting Amelia, and of his crassness, sometimes highly embarrassing even to her, as he pushed her career. He came on so strong that many people could not stand to be in the same room with him. "If he went to a dogfight, he'd have to be one of the dogs," observed an acquaintance. Photographers dubbed him "the lens louse" because he always elbowed in on coverage of his famous wife. Anne Morrow Lindbergh confided ominously to her diary in 1933, "Amelia Earhart's husband hovering," while describing the aviator herself as "a shaft of white coming out of a blue room."[8]

Female aviators concurred with Anne Morrow Lindbergh's assessment of G.P. Jacqueline Cochran, perhaps the generation's most talented and versatile pilot, recounted how patronizing Putnam was to her when she first met him, saying, "Well, little girl, what's your ambition in flying?" Cochran testily replied, "To put your wife in the shade, sir." Elinor Smith, an aspiring pilot who had learned to fly at age twelve and held the women's solo endurance record, was convinced that Putnam had deliberately sabotaged her career by making sure that she did not get certain endorsements and contracts. Florence ("Pancho") Barnes, a free-spirited California stunt pilot, went even further, calling Putnam a "Svengali" and complaining of Earhart, whom she did not like, "She was a goddamned robot. Putnam would wind her up and she'd go and do what he said." Barnes's reaction was extreme. Most flyers, and many of their friends, absolved her and tolerated him.[9]

Whatever George Palmer Putnam's character flaws (and they were legion), he was enormously important to Amelia Earhart's career. "I know I'm lucky to have him, for I never could do it without his help. He takes care of everything," Amelia conceded before leaving on her round-the-world flight. If Earhart's interests were more in the aviation field, and Putnam's in the direction of publicity, celebrity, and the lifestyles of the rich and famous, they nevertheless managed to strike a balance in their personal and professional partnership. "I'm a very good passenger," said G.P. "He is a very good front seat driver," replied Earhart. As aviator Fay Gillis Wells recalled later, "Amelia described it herself as a marriage of convenience. But they both had a wonderful zest for living; and I think they both respected each other. She knew that he was most helpful to her, and he knew he had a marvelous commodity."[10]

George Palmer Putnam was born in 1887 in Rye, New York, into a prominent, but not especially wealthy, New England family whose name is still associated with the publishing firm G. P. Putnam's Sons. "My father was a publisher, and his father before him. My earliest recollections are of books; and authors, whom I have never held in proper awe since." He attended Harvard College and the University of California at Berkeley but was not graduated from either institution. Choosing not to enter the family business, he set off at age twenty-one to Bend, Oregon, in 1909 to make his own way. Over the next six years, he bought and edited the local newspaper, the *Bend Bulletin*, and served as the town's mayor. He also dabbled in politics at the gubernatorial level. In 1911, he married Dorothy Binney, a daughter in the family that had made its fortune with Binney and Smith Crayola crayons. They had two sons: David Binney Putnam (born 1913) and George Palmer Putnam, Jr. (born 1921).[11]

When World War I broke out, Putnam enlisted, but he did not serve overseas. The death of his older brother in the worldwide influenza pandemic in 1918 caused him to change his plans of returning to Oregon. Instead, he took his brother's place at the family publishing house, G. P. Putnam's Sons, and settled his family into a spacious mansion in his hometown of Rye. The publishing world showcased the talent he had already shown in Oregon for surrounding himself with lively and interesting people, throwing good parties, and generally being in the middle of everything. He was especially drawn to adventure and exploration stories, for which the public displayed an insatiable appetite in the 1920s. For example, G. P. Putnam's Sons published Lindbergh's *We* (1927), the phenomenal best seller describing the Atlantic solo, and Richard Byrd's *Skyward* (1928), an account of Byrd's exploration by plane of the North Pole.

But Putnam had aspirations toward being an explorer and author himself. "I practiced what I preached. It seemed inappropriate to promote books about exploration without doing a bit of exploration myself. So I did." In 1926, he undertook a six-month expedition to Greenland, writing syndicated front-page stories on the voyage for the *New York Times*, and the next summer he organized a scientific expedition to Canada's Baffin Island. A fellow traveler on one of these adventures captured Putnam's seemingly insatiable need to be at the center of the action with this only slightly overdrawn characterization: "George would have stopped in the middle of a rotten plank over a chasm a hundred feet deep to broadcast his reaction to a waiting world."[12]

One offshoot of his explorer phase was a series of adventure books for young readers. His twelve-year-old son David inaugurated the series with *David Goes Voyaging* (1925), a description of being the junior member on William Beebe's expedition to the Galapagos Islands, followed by *David Goes to Greenland* (1926) and *David Goes to Baffin Island* (1927). Another book by an adventurous young author was sixteen-year-old Bradford Washburn's *Among the Alps with Bradford* (1927), the story of the teenager's hiking and climbing in Switzerland and France. In a quirk of fate, Washburn was approached to serve as the navigator for Earhart's round-the-world flight in 1937 because of this prior connection with Putnam, but he was never formally offered the position.[13]

The success of Putnam's publishing ventures in adventuring, especially the Lindbergh and Byrd books, had drawn him increasingly into aviation, as had his association with the production of the successful aviation film *Wings* (1927), which won the first Academy Award for best picture. In 1928, he heard of a possible transatlantic flight involving a woman under the sponsorship of Amy Phipps Guest. Soon he was involved in finding the "right sort of girl" to make the flight, although both he and Hilton Railey claim credit for discovering the young Boston settlement worker named Miss Earhart. After the successful *Friendship* flight, Putnam continued to advise Amelia on her fledgling career, while maintaining his usual full plate of publishing and promotional ventures. Putnam remained in his family's publishing firm until 1930, when it merged with another firm. He joined the publishing venture of Brewer and Warren, but left in 1932 to become chairman of the editorial board of Paramount, a New York–based job of somewhat vague responsibilities, which he held until 1935. But long before then, Putnam was basically functioning as a full-time manager and promoter of his aviator wife.[14]

What George Putnam did for Amelia Earhart was part old-time promoter (as if she were a boxing star or polar explorer), part press agent (writing and handing out the press releases), and part public relations counsel, a new profession in the 1920s and '30s. As epitomized by Edward Bernays, public relations was a new way of managing the news—not just getting publicity but constructing and manipulating events in order to get positive results. Putnam, totally committed to the public image of his client, was very much a manager and manipulator of events, always seeking an excuse to get his wife's name in the paper.[15] "Here I am jumping through hoops just like the little white horse in the circus," Earhart complained during a particularly strenuous trip in 1931.[16]

"In the routine meaning of the term I was, I suppose, Amelia Earhart's manager," wrote George Palmer Putnam. "Philosophically, as has been said, she felt no human being of normal intelligence should be *managed* by anyone else. Temperamentally she had a healthy distaste for the implication of being led around by the hand. Yet no client of any counselor ever received counsel more reasonably— or, on occasion, refused with more firmness to act on it!" Perhaps Putnam was thinking of the time that he had ordered a batch of children's hats embellished with a facsimile of her signature, and she had absolutely refused to have anything to do with them because they were so cheaply made. Or of how she, fearful of not living up to advance billing, would never announce her flights beforehand, sheer torture to a publicity freak like George Putnam. But he may have had his way anyhow: three of her major flights (the Atlantic solo, a 1933 transcontinental speed record, and the 1935 solo from Hawaii) all began on Friday, finished on Saturday, and thus made the front pages in the Sunday newspaper editions with the widest circulations.[17]

One of Putnam's other main functions as Amelia's manager and promoter was raising money for her flights. "I try to make my flying self-supporting," she told reporters after a record-breaking flight in 1935. "I could not fly otherwise." She never quite did break even, so tapping benefactors and taking advantage of business opportunities were a must. Here Putnam's promotional skills and wide-ranging connections in the worlds of entertainment, sports, and business were enormously useful. "After all, record flying is terribly expensive and we have to accept legitimate returns when we can get them," Putnam once said to business associate Paul Mantz. Amelia used similar words in the wake of her 1932 solo when she told reporters that she would capitalize "in any legitimate way that comes to hand. Any woman who wishes to should be able to do so without stigma." But as Ruth Nichols noted, women were at a disadvantage when it came to raising money: "The people who could finance these undertakings have not believed as we have and have not been willing to back us financially. It has been much easier for men to get backing, for the public has more confidence in the men fliers." Here is where George probably made a crucial difference in making sure that "your client's public-character wife" (as Earhart once jokingly referred to herself) had as many opportunities as comparable men.[18]

In some ways it is surprising that Amelia Earhart endorsed anything at all after her first experience. In return for a $1,500 endorsement fee, Amelia Earhart "wickedly" (her word) appeared in an ad for Lucky Strike cigarettes after the 1928 flight. The copy read, "Lucky Strikes were the cigarettes carried on the 'Friendship' when she crossed the Atlantic."[19] Amelia Earhart did not in fact smoke, but she wanted to make a contribution toward Commander Richard E. Byrd's upcoming Antarctic expedition in return for his support of her trip. Byrd publicly called Earhart's gesture "an act of astonishing generosity," but others of the general public, for whom smoking by women was still unacceptable in the 1920s, were not so positive. One irate correspondent wrote Earhart, "I suppose you drink too." (She did neither.) The adverse publicity cost the newest aviation celebrity a columnist's job at *McCall's*, but Ray Long at *Cosmopolitan* quickly signed her on. She never endorsed cigarettes again, or alcohol.[20]

Endorsements were big business in advertising and product promotion, but they worked only if done carefully. The most successful ads were ones where "big names," well-known public figures with upstanding reputations, had logical links to the product; less successful, in fact almost totally discredited by the 1930s, were Hollywood types of celebrities who indiscriminately endorsed one product after another with no logical or appropriate connection.[21] Amelia Earhart was often in demand, and she endorsed or appeared in support of the following products: Kodak film, Pratt & Whitney Wasp engines,[22] Stanavo engine oil,[23] Franklin and Hudson automobiles, Lucky Strike cigarettes, women's clothing and luggage, Time Saver note cards and stationery,[24] and a mail-order kitchen firm. The endorsements of aviation products no doubt resulted in contributions of products and services to the latest Earhart-Putnam air venture, and clothing and accessories plugs were logical considering her yearly appearance on the best-dressed lists. However, the endorsement that Putnam arranged for mail-order kitchen cabinets in exchange for a set of the products for a new Hollywood house they were building was not very believable; how much time did Amelia Earhart spend in the kitchen? Friends like aviation writer Carl B. Allen thought that this was one case where G.P. went too far.[25]

Less controversial, and more in line with her public image, was Amelia Earhart Air-Light Luggage. Her mother recalled that Amelia "happened to be talking one day to the man she knew who was designing luggage and she made such sensible suggestions that he asked her to give him her ideas." The result was an association with the Orenstein Trunk Corporation of Newark, New Jersey, which began in 1933, whereby Earhart received royalty for her ideas and the use of her name. A press release called it "the first truly practical and genuine airplane luggage," able to provide both extreme lightness and great strength through its use of three-plywood aircraft veneer wood suggested by Earhart. Alice Hughes, fashion authority of the Hearst newspapers, commented: "Everything is one-third lighter in weight than the usual travel equipment. Any who have had to pay 80 cents a pound for excess airplane baggage will appreciate this thoughtfulness on the part of Miss Earhart." Even though not that many Americans flew for business or vacation yet, she tapped a potential market for aviation-related accessories that could be used in other forms of travel.[26]

❦The publicity for the luggage prominently featured the aviator. Macy's did a window display which included a fully equipped model of a pilot's cabin with the displayed luggage and pictures of Amelia. Dressed in her customary traveling outfit of slacks, plaid shirt, and silk scarf, she posed for publicity shots loading the luggage into an airplane. The text stressed how she had adapted airplane technology and expertise to the design of luggage: "Amelia Earhart, whose knowledge of things aeronautical was un-questioned, drew on available scientific data and from her own experience in airplane and other modes of travel designed the first practical and genuine aeroplane luggage."[27] Few things better capture the changes under way in aviation than a record-breaking solo pilot designing luggage for the everyday use of the airplane passenger. The luggage is still being manufactured today, its appeal undiminished de-spite the fact that its namesake died in a plane crash.

Amelia Earhart also designed and marketed a line of clothing under her name in 1933 and 1934. Why clothing? "I just don't like shopping very much," she told an interviewer, adding, "I hate ruffles, and at the price I could pay that was all I could buy. So I decided to design clothes. They are nothing ex-citing, just good lines and good materials for women who lead active lives." Even though the models were promoted as sports clothes, she preferred the term "active clothes": "This is an era of feminine ac-tivity. The stay-at-home and the hammock girl are gone. Modern women are strenuously active."[28]

As was the case with the luggage, there was a clear rationale behind the association. The clothes had many links to flying, such as using parachute silk for fabric or fashioning buttonholes and fasteners in the shape of airplane hardware. "I have always believed that clothes are terribly important in every woman's life," Earhart said, "and I also believe that there is much of beauty in aviation—color and line that is exclusive to the air, which I have attempted to express in my sports clothes." Again and again the designer turned to aviation for inspiration: "I tried to put the freedom that is in flying into the clothes. And the efficiency too." The logo featured the exhaust trail of a plane bisecting her name.[29]

This foray into "air-minded fashions" turned into "one of the hardest strains she ever went through because she was doing so much at that time," according to her mother. Earhart did not just lend her name and a few rough sketches and ideas. She was very much involved in the development of the twenty-five designs which constituted the collection. When interviewers came to her office suite at the Seymour Hotel, Amelia was likely to be surrounded by clotheshorses, fabric samples, pins (and fan mail, over-flowing in a corner). She did not, however, personally stitch up the models. The clothes were manufactured by four New York firms, with hats provided by a fifth. They were sold only in special Amelia Earhart Shops within department stores: Macy's had the New York franchise, Marshall Field held it in Chicago, and Jordan Marsh in Boston. This arrangement, common today, was unusual at the time. Perhaps it was modeled on Macy's Cinema Shop, which opened in 1933 to sell reproductions of clothing seen in current films, complete with the name of the star and the picture in which she wore the original.[30]

The advertisements for the Amelia Earhart line in *Women's Wear Daily* and women's magazines often featured the aviator herself modeling the clothes, and doing quite a professional job, too. The designs were indeed simple, practical, and comfortable, with touches usually reserved for men's tailoring. These fashions were geared to the middle-class shopper, not someone interested in haute couture. A dress cost around $30, slacks $16.75, and a tweed suit went for $55. Besides the unusual aviation details, the blouses, jackets, and skirts were sold separately. This, too, was a novelty.[31]

Yet by the end of 1934, this experiment had failed, the victim not just of the Depression but of the vagaries of the women's fashion industry. The fashion industry was just too entrenched, even before the Depression had cut back on the disposable income of the female consumer, for a neophyte like Amelia Earhart to break into and succeed in this highly competitive, volatile market. Amelia and George didn't lose any money on the venture, but they don't seem to have made any either.

But the venture was hardly a total failure. The line of clothing brought the aviator visibility, it reflected the quality that the public associated with her name, and it allowed her to promote her view of the new active womanhood. Women could do things in these clothes, and that was precisely what she had in mind: "I made my clothes to have good long shirt-tails, that wouldn't come loose no matter if the wearer took time to stand on her head." Here, as in so many other areas, she was definitely ahead of her times.[32]

No commercial link in Earhart's career took up as much of her time and energy as her fashion designing. Other promotions and endorsements were usually one-shot events or plugs designed for maximum publicity. "If she could find people she believed in, representing something she believed in, which would benefit from the news she could create," her manager rationalized, "she was willing and glad to make that news help underwrite her activities." She christened a new plane owned by the Parker Pen Company, the Goodyear dirigible *Resolute*, and stylish automobiles like the Essex Terraplane. She had her vision tested on top of the newly opened Empire State Building in 1931 as part of a promotional campaign by the Better Vision Institute. She went diving in a deep-sea outfit in Long Island Sound, a stunt which was covered by the *New York Times* and then written up by Earhart as one of her *Cosmopolitan* articles.[33] As might be expected, George Putnam's promotional talents lay behind most, if not all, of these stunts. As he cooed about his wife's demonstration of a parachute jump, "Nothing I have ever touched has, proportionally, attracted such wide-spread national publicity. It has proved a 'natural.' Practically every major paper in the country has carried pictures or a story."[34]

Most of these promotions took up time Amelia would rather have spent flying, so she was intrigued by a scheme George cooked up in 1931 with the Beech-Nut Packing Company. This promotion involved a twenty-one-day cross-country trip in an autogiro, a windmill type of plane which was a forerunner of the modern helicopter. The autogiro had wide commercial possibilities, mainly in advertising, and Earhart's autogiro had "Beech-Nut" written prominently on the fuselage. In addition to the national publicity generated by the trip, the need to refuel every two hours meant frequent stops and local visibility. Earhart remembered fondly the warm hospitality and genuine friendliness which greeted her and her mechanic in the seventy-six places they put down in their long tour. But even if it was fun, it was still grueling work, especially the promotional aspects. "But, alas, my autogyro could not talk, or eat chicken, or speak on the radio, or be interviewed—and its pilot, after a manner, could."[35]

Considering her husband's association with Paramount Pictures, it was probably inevitable that Earhart would find her way to Hollywood. George and Amelia were very much part of the Southern California scene, which was as great a place for flying as it was for making movies. George spent a fair amount of time on the West Coast in connection with his Paramount job, and the Putnams counted film stars like Mary Pickford and Douglas Fairbanks as their friends. On several occasions, Earhart was photographed with stars such as Cary Grant, Marlene Dietrich, Tallulah Bankhead, and Gary Cooper (a mutual promotional scheme, no doubt), and it was rumored in February 1933 that she might become an advisor on upcoming aviation films. Carl Laemmle of Universal Studios had gone even further, trying to convince Earhart that she "owed it to her public" to go into pictures, but she just laughed it off. The only pictures she would have considered, she said, were ones that would advance the cause of women in flying or one in which "they let me play my unromantic self, slacks, engine grease and all."[36] But she was never really tempted to try her hand at acting, no doubt to her husband's disappointment. She simply concluded that Hollywood "isn't my sort of thing" and that "I'm a transport flyer, and I'd better stick to my plane!"[37]

There are many parallels between Amelia Earhart's life as a popular heroine and those of Hollywood stars: cultivating a public image; attending carefully staged promotional events; endorsing selected products; being widely photographed and written about; working very hard at what one does. Like Bette Davis or Katharine Hepburn, Amelia Earhart could not walk down the street unnoticed; like the facts about Hollywood stars, details about her personal life and opinions were picked up by the eager media.

Another similarity was receiving a huge amount of mail. In the single month of April 1928 Clara Bow, the "It" girl, received 33,727 letters, some simply addressed to "It, Hollywood, California." In Hollywood, the volume of mail was so large that stars could not possibly answer it themselves, so the studios created elaborate publicity departments to handle the correspondence, most of which consisted of requests for autographs or pictures. Very early the studio executives realized that while expensive, such promotion built goodwill and encouraged fan loyalty.[38]

Just as fans wrote to their favorite stars in Hollywood, so young (and old) admirers wrote to Amelia Earhart about their flying aspirations. The first inkling occurred after her 1928 flight: "I never knew that a 'public character' (that, Heaven help me, apparently is my fate since the flight) could be the target of so much mail," said Amelia with a sigh. Four secretaries were necessary to deal with the telegrams, letters of congratulation, commercial offers, proposals of marriage, and crank mail that poured in.[39]

For the rest of her career, Earhart kept up an enormous correspondence, especially after such record-breaking fights as the 1932 solo. Responding promptly and efficiently to fan mail was an important aspect of being a popular heroine, one which the aviator actually enjoyed. Characteristically, according to her husband, "she read nearly everything that came to her." Inundated by so much mail, she tried to keep her sense of humor. She called her personal papers her "peppers" and had files marked "bunk" (for all the songs, poems, and accolades that people sent in) and "cousins" (for those who tried to establish an often fictive family connection).[40]

But the demands of her public often cut into her ability to stay in touch with friends. "I do not have much time to write letters," she told an old friend. "I dream that by working very hard I'll have some time later to watch sunsets." She confessed to an aviation buddy in early 1934, "To take a year in answering a letter is about my average rate just now. My friends suffer most, because I am continually shoving their letters aside telling myself they will understand delay while a business correspondent will not. I know my theory is unjust, for I value friends more than I do the butcher, baker, or candlestick maker, worthy souls though they may be. What to do about regulating my life and letters, I know not."[41]

But she did, at least, keep in touch with her mother and sister, often dashing off letters in the midst of her cross-country travels. The responsibility she had already assumed for her family before the 1928 flight continued once she became a successful and relatively affluent person. But the tone changed. She became patronizing, opinionated, and dogmatic as she told family members how to conduct their lives in a way she never let anyone rule hers. The now-prominent daughter treated her mother, Amy Otis Earhart, like a small child. Relationships with her younger sister, Muriel, with whom Amy lived in Medford, were not much better.[42]

Amelia was now supporting her mother entirely and helping her sister out financially, and she seemed to think that her financial contributions allowed her to interfere as well. "Please throw away rags and get things you need on my account at Filenes," she told her mother immediately after the 1928 flight. "I can do it now, and the pleasure is mine." She was still badgering her mother about clothes in 1935. "Please remember you and Pidge attract attention as my relatives so spare me blowsies. I'd prefer you to get a few simple decent clothes, both of you, not awful cheapies, so people who don't look below the surface won't have anything to converse about." Amelia, of course, was correct that people would think she was selfish if her family went around looking poor, but the peremptory tone of her request betrayed an edginess and impatience with her family that were characteristic of her dealings with them in this period.[43]

Another recurring source of recrimination was what Amelia called "the family failing about money." Sometimes she sent only half what her mother requested because "I thought if I sent the whole you would spend it on someone else and not have anything left for yourself by the first of next month." She reminded her mother, "What I send you is what I myself earn and it does not come from GP. I feel the church gets some of what should go to living expenses and I have no wish to continue that to Pidge's loss."[44]

It is difficult to excuse the offensive and patronizing tone of these letters, but it does seem possible that the stress of her public career adversely affected Amelia's ability to relate freely and unconditionally to her family. Perhaps success did go to her head, but more likely it was the constant oppression of feeling that everybody wanted a piece of her. For self-protection, she had to get away from the demands of people, even her family, echoing artist Georgia O'Keeffe's plaintive cry "I have to keep some of myself or I wouldn't have anything left to give."[45] Often George was left with the task of remembering cards and flowers on birthdays, sending along monthly support checks, and settling petty squabbles and misunderstandings with Amelia's family. These responsibilities continued after her death.[46]

"Today, if you ever figure in any unusual exploit, be it a flight, a voyage in a small boat, or, say, a channel swim," noted Amelia, paraphrasing Alice in Wonderland, "'There's a publisher close behind you who is treading on your heels.'" Of all the duties surrounding being a public figure, the aviator seems to have derived the least satisfaction from writing. She had written poetry all her life but was unable to transfer her affinity for verse into the autobiography and general nonfiction required of a public figure out to keep her name in the news. Moreover, she found the deadline conditions under which she had to churn out her prose especially disruptive to good writing. As a result, she was rarely satisfied with anything she produced.[47]

The success of Charles Lindbergh's *We* made it inevitable that Amelia Earhart would try her hand at a similar account after her June 1928 flight. (Would the book be called "She"? wondered one skeptic, who accused Putnam of cashing in on the Lindbergh connection.) Poor Amelia quickly concluded that "the hop . . . was rather easier than the writing." With a great deal of editorial guidance from Putnam, she finished a manuscript in three weeks while staying in Rye. "Finally the little book is done, such as it is." She was rather unsure of the "airworthiness of the manuscript" but sounded like a kid at the end of school: "Tomorrow I am free to fly." Her reward from the drudgery of "writers' cramp"? A cross-country vagabond in the plane purchased from Lady Heath. But even that vacation soon found its way into print, as one of her first articles as aviation editor for *Cosmopolitan*. At times it must have seemed as if nothing she did didn't need to be recycled for public consumption. No wonder her letter writing suffered.[48]

20 Hrs. 40 Min. truly was an instant book: Earhart finished it on August 25, and it was in the bookstores by September 10. Earhart and her publisher, G. P. Putnam's Sons (not coincidentally her future husband's family firm), thus reaped the potential profits while her name was still fresh in the public mind after her June flight.[49]

A slightly different pattern prevailed for *The Fun of It*, the bulk of which was written in the winter of 1931–32. Its subtitle, *Random Records of My Own Flying and of Women in Aviation*, captured the hodge-podge quality of the book, much of which merely reworked material from earlier published writing. But no doubt Putnam had impressed on Earhart the need for something fresh, like a new book, to attract publicity and keep her name before the public. Once Amelia informed George of her decision to try the Atlantic solo, he timed the release of the book to the projected first week of her homecoming. "Here, at the request of the publishers, is a final chapter describing the flight itself—a postscript from overseas," she told her readers. To capitalize further on the flight, each book contained a small phonographic recording of part of the radio broadcast Earhart had made from London, a very catchy G.P. promotional gimmick.[50]

Both these books received generally good reviews,[51] although sales never approached the Lindbergh book. In fact, none of the later aviation or adventure books did; once again, his reception was unique. Readers enjoyed the autobiographical details Earhart supplied and gained a sense of what learning to fly was like. As usual, the author sprinkled her texts with feminist reminders that women, too, were flying. But in general Earhart's prose was pedestrian and lacking in drama. The books, already printed in very large type and illustrated by many photographs (often the best part), seemed padded with extraneous chapters and recycled material. She was just going through the motions expected of a public figure, and under a deadline no less.

Earhart's magazine articles were somewhat livelier, although they, too, had the sense of being written out of necessity rather than inspiration. *Cosmopolitan* expected one article an issue, so the new aviation editor dutifully circled the fourth day of each month to remind her to meet the dreaded deadline. There were just so many ways that she could write about women and flying, flying and women, women and aviation, however. (On the other hand, she very much enjoyed answering the mail addressed to her care of the magazine.) In addition, there were numerous assignments for fluff pieces in other magazines that George diligently lined up, like their joint "My Husband / My Wife" for *Redbook* or Amelia's article on their summer vacation at a Wyoming dude ranch. Probably the best articles that Amelia Earhart wrote—or rather, the ones truest to her approach to aviation and life—were not the artificially jaunty pieces turned out for national magazines but the longer descriptions of her flights published in serious publications like *National Geographic*. Here she could just tell the story of her flight, what she had actually done, rather than have to entertain an audience.[52]

Her hardest deadlines involved the syndicated first-person accounts she had to write immediately following each of her record-breaking flights. These very lucrative contracts (the *New York Times* paid $20,000 in 1928 for the story of the *Friendship*, although her part of the fee went back into flight expenses) were the bread and butter of the expensive sport of record breaking. They were also a staple of journalism at the time. G.P. was enormously successful in lining up exclusive syndication deals for each of his wife's major flights and even for some of her minor ones as well.[53]

In order for these articles to be timely, they had to be written almost the moment after her plane landed. As soon as she met with the newsreel photographers and gave a few brief remarks to reporters (not too much, however, because that would detract from the value of her own account), she retired to knock out her story. "Without waiting to change from her flying togs . . . Miss Earhart sat down at her portable typewriter when she reached the Seymour and started pounding out her personal story of the flight for the *New York Herald Tribune*," said an account in that paper after a record flight from Mexico City to Newark in 1935. "Her only concession to the strain to which she had been subjected was to order a chicken and lettuce sandwich and a glass of buttermilk sent up to her room. She nibbled one and sipped the other while she wrote."[54] If these postflight accounts were more straightforward than thrilling, they reflected the careful preparation she put into her flights, her tendency not to sensationalize or overdramatize her story, and her inevitable weariness at having to write immediately after the strain of a grueling long-distance flight.

The aviator felt slightly more at home on the radio, where she was a frequent commentator and lecturer. She must have been good at it because the Columbia Broadcasting System presented her with a medal for distinguished contributions to radio art in June 1932. Many of the major events in her public career were broadcast: the welcome home parade in New York City in 1928; the first full description of that flight from Madison Square Garden; her speeches to the National Geographic Society in 1932 and 1935. Perhaps her most exciting radio transmission was the live hookup from London over CBS network after her transatlantic solo in May 1932, although her mother and Muriel claimed the quality was so poor they could hardly recognize her voice. She also appeared on such shows as the Friday night aviation series on WABC and on "The Inside Story," which included a dramatization and interview conducted by the popular radio commentator Edwin C. Hill. Twice she broadcast live from the air: in May 1933, from eight different points over New York City on WABC, and in January 1935, when she talked to her husband via commercial radio while flying solo between Hawaii and Oakland. Radio was well entrenched in American households by the 1930s, but hearing celebrities describe their adventures was still enough of a novelty to count as entertainment. It was yet another way that links were forged between a public figure and the American public at large.[55]

But in the days before television, the lecture circuit, even more so than the newsreels or radio, was the principle means by which popular figures reached the public. Here was a chance for citizens in Des Moines, Iowa, or Tacoma, Washington, to see what polar explorer Richard Byrd or humorist Will Rogers or first lady Eleanor Roosevelt was like in person. They could hear about the latest exploits of journalist Dorothy Thompson or photographer Margaret Bourke-White. Rather then the vicarious experience of radio or newsreels, lectures provided an opportunity to connect in person with the most in-fluential political, social, and cultural leaders of their times, at least for one night.

Of course, for a public figure to draw a crowd, he or she had to have something to say. Public figures were only as good as their most recent exploit or accomplishment. Whenever Amelia Earhart's stan-dard lecture on "Adventures in Flying" began to go stale, she would do something like make another record-breaking flight or write a new book to give it fresh material. Earhart's talks were geared to a gen-eral audience and avoided controversial subjects such as pacifism or politics, which she was freer to dis-cuss in interviews. But she always included references to women in aviation as part of her general talk. Her ever-helpful coach G.P. tutored her to speak from note cards and synchronize her talk to the ac-companying newsreel footage, and he taught her how to use a pointer without turning her back to the audience, how to ration time, and the importance of crisp endings. He also kept her posted in their nightly telephone conversations about what kind of crowd she would be addressing (a women's club luncheon, a large public speech in the high school auditorium, a tea or social) and whether she had spo-ken in that locality before.[56]

Life on the lecture tour was a real grind of "one-night stands" and "one hotel after another." Earhart preferred to drive to her engagements, rather then go by train; occasionally she flew. Although she al-ways reserved the time before her talk to compose herself, she usually was willing afterward to attend an informal reception, sign autographs ("Autographing, I discover, is a national mania"), or submit to the obligatory interview with the local newspaper. She often left a lecture around midnight and then drove on to her next engagement; that way she could get a good night's sleep wherever she was going. "I drove here all the way and arrived about four thirty A.M.," she told her mother from Iowa. "It was a gorgeous night and I thought I'd rather sleep for a few hours after I reached Sioux City than to get up at an early hour and drive from somewhere along the way to arrive for luncheon." Always the insatiable tourist, she noted how the roads had improved since she and her mother made their cross-country journey in 1924: "They are elegant now and almost as well marked as California." Usually she was on her own, although occasionally she hooked up with her husband. "G.P. meets me at Bowling Green," she wrote her moth-er from Knoxville. "I am not sure whether it will be more or less strenuous with him."[57]

It is hard to imagine anything more strenuous than these lecture tours. During one stretch in Octo-ber 1933, she delivered twenty-three talks in twenty-five days; she logged 7,000 miles by car, much of it alone, in just over six weeks. In 1935, one biographer counted 135 stage appearances, before total audi-ences estimated at 80,000. Between September 30 and November 3, 1935, she crisscrossed her way from Youngstown, Ohio, to Michigan, on to Minnesota, through Nebraska, into Iowa, to Chicago, then down to Galesburg and Decatur, into Indiana, back up to Michigan, back down to Chicago, off to Mis-souri and Kansas, back to Indiana, finally finishing in Wilmette, Illinois.[58] She earned between $250 and $300 for each lecture, although she was willing to take less for a charitable cause. Seven or eight lectures in a week totaled close to $2,400, a tidy sum in Depression America. Lecturing became very quickly her major source of income.[59]

As might be expected, such lecture tours took their toll. Her mother sometimes traveled with her and saw the pressure firsthand: "I remember again and again after evenings when she gave a talk and answered questions, and people thoughtlessly arranged a reception for her afterward or neighbors and friends pressed in to speak or to talk to her, she came home dead tired, saying to me, 'No talkee, mother, my cocoa, good night.'" The stress of the 1935 tour landed her in the hospital with a flare-up of an old sinus problem and pleurisy, and she was uncharacteristically bedridden for ten days, probably one of the longest stretches she stayed put in her entire life.[60]

Not surprisingly, husband and wife often had diametrically opposed perspectives on these lecture tours. George could write blithely during the middle of one such tour, "She, herself, is about mid-way in an extraordinarily successful lecture tour which is bringing her before over 100 major audiences throughout the country—to all of which, of course, she is preaching the pleasures and advantages of flying." Privately Amelia had a less upbeat take on the whole lecture process, calling her schedule at various times "the most strenuous lecture engagement ever undertaken," "signed for the treadmill," and "unescapable." George's central role in scheduling, indeed overscheduling, the tours is clear from this note to her mother: "They were much more intensive than I had planned because the management [G.P.] kept trying to squeeze in more, and in these times I thought I might as well do as much and get as much as I could. Well, anyway they are over." No wonder Amelia loved the solitude of flying—the one time she was free from the demands of her life as a public figure.[61]

It is ironic that this world-famous aviator spent more time on the ground talking about flying than in the air, where she wanted to be. Luckily she did not mind public speaking. "I think it's only fair to say that she like anyone enjoyed applause," remarked her sister, Muriel, who occasionally accompanied her on tour, "and when she had completed a lecture and had a crowded audience and had them really on the edge of their chairs, you might say, enjoying it, I think she enjoyed that." But she never craved the public stature of a celebrity. She merely wanted what celebrity made possible. Fellow aviator Fay Gillis Wells confirmed that her friend had no compulsion to be the center of attention: "Some people exhibit an aura of charisma; a brilliance lights up, and bells ring—they are center stage. Amelia wasn't like that. She didn't mind the recognition, when it was earned, but she didn't want to be on stage unless it was essential to reach her goal. If it was money she needed, she would lecture her heart out to get the dues to pay the bills."[62]

The remarkable thing, of course, was how Amelia Earhart managed to conceal from each audience any of the strain, boredom, or stress that had gotten her to that particular podium on that particular day in Anywhere, U.S.A. Clearly she took pride in what she was doing and took her role as a goodwill ambassador for modern aviation and women's rights very seriously. Even though she was not a wildly charismatic speaker, she was effective at establishing a rapport with her audience, and she knew how to work a crowd.

A talk she gave to the Daughters of the American Revolution in 1933 confirms her ease on the platform. The transcript is liberally punctuated by the annotations "laughter" and "applause" as she charmed her audience with self-deprecating stories about her celebrity. For example, she opened with the time a young boy announced after seeing her poster for an upcoming lecture, "Daddy, daddy, Colonel Lindbergh's Mother is going to lecture here." Toward the beginning of the lecture, she self-consciously yet humorously gave the audience the "special sermon" she usually preached to women on aviation: "It isn't very long and I might as well preach it here because I feel that the effort will be coming on me," an introduction that provoked laughter from the crowd. She then proceeded to hold them spellbound with the story of her 1932 Atlantic flight.[63]

Further insights into her lecturing come from the recollections of those who heard her speak. "She won the people of Vermont which is not an easy thing to do," noted one satisfied customer. "We all thought Lindbergh was a marvel but our 'Amelia' has shown the world what a woman can do." Another satisfied customer remembered how, when the newsreel she was showing of a postflight appearance suddenly turned jerky, she quickly ad-libbed that it really wasn't her first pair of high heels! Alice Kalousdian came under Amelia Earhart's spell at a 1932 Hunter College appearance: "There is nothing in the tilt of her head, or in the warm glow of her eyes that suggests the much interviewed, photographed, and 'autographed' personality. . . . Not for a moment has she the air of one who is being talked about and looked at. She listens, instead, like a spectator of her own career." Many people were probably just as interested in seeing and meeting her as in whatever she had to say. "Her smile and her gracious femininity were unforgettable," recalled one, "but what she said I don't recall."[64]

By 1935, Amelia Earhart had taken her place as a major aviation celebrity and as one of America's best-known and admired women. She had been in the public eye for seven years. Few of the popular heroines, male or female, who flashed briefly into public consciousness in the 1920s and 1930s and then just as quickly disappeared could make such a claim to longevity. But few of them devoted as much energy and hard work to maintaining their public reputation as she did. Nor did most of them have as hardworking and persistent a publicist as G. P. Putnam.

Whether Amelia Earhart would have been able to maintain her stature indefinitely without the unsolved mystery of her disappearance remains unclear. Ironically, this popular heroine who worked so hard at that role in the 1930s now effortlessly generates reams and reams of publicity more than seventy years after her death, and all without George Putnam cranking the handle of the publicity machine.

Notes

1   Gertrude Ederle, quoted in *New York Times*, August 7, 1926, p. 1; Amelia Earhart, "Questions I Have Met," *Aeronautic Review* (February 1929), p. 7.

2   Orrin E. Klapp, "Hero Worship in America," *American Sociological Review* 14 (February 1949), pp. 61–62.

3   Ederle returned home to a tumultuous New York ticker tape parade and received commercial offers totaling close to a million dollars, but she was unable to cash in on them. She toured vaudeville houses with a swimming act but had no success converting her athletic prowess into a Hollywood career. Never bitter, she became a swimming instructor in New York and never married. For more on Ederle, see "How a Girl Beat Leander at the Hero Game," *Literary Digest* 90 (August 21, 1926), pp. 52–67.
Ruth Elder was also treated as a heroine, honored by the National Women's Party and offered a screen test in Hollywood. She made several silent movies, went on tour, and made a lot of money. But she spent it just as quickly. Even though she continued to fly for sport (she competed in the 1929 Powder Puff Derby and was a charter member of the Ninety-Nines), she dropped out of sight in the 1930s. Married six times, including to the New York socialite Walter Camp, Jr., she died in 1978. For more on Elder, see Judy Lomax, *Women of the Air* (New York: Dodd, Mead, 1987), pp. 65–66, and Kathleen Brooks-Pazmany, *United States Women in Aviation, 1919–1929* (Washington, DC: Smithsonian Institution Press, 1991), pp. 21–22.

4   George Palmer Putnam, *Soaring Wings: A Biography of Amelia Earhart* (New York: Harcourt, Brace, 1939), p. 190. Or, as he said on the same page, "In itself, being a celebrity is very hard work indeed."

5   Amelia Earhart, quoted in Universal Service clipping, May 9, 1935, found in Clarence Strong Williams Papers, Schlesinger Library, Harvard University.

6   *Newsweek*, January 19, 1935, quoted in Doris L. Rich, *Amelia Earhart: A Biography* (Washington DC: Smithsonian Institution Press, 1989), p. 196; Amelia Earhart to Bert Kinner, February 1933, quoted ibid., p. 155; Universal Service clipping, May 9, 1935, found in Clarence Strong Williams Papers, Schlesinger Library, Harvard University.

7   Bobbi Trout, quoted in Rich, *Amelia Earhart*, p. 119; Mary S. Lovell, *The Sound of Wings: The Life of Amelia Earhart* (New York: St. Martin's Press, 1989), p. xvii; Elinor Smith, *Aviatrix* (New York: Harcourt Brace Jovanovich, 1981), pp. 73–74.

8   Lovell, *Sound of Wings*, p. 81; Anne Morrow Lindbergh, *Locked Rooms and Open Doors: Diaries and Letters, 1933–1935* (New York: Harcourt Brace Jovanovich, 1974), p. 5.

9   Jacqueline Cochran and Maryann Bucknum Brinley, *Jackie Cochran: An Autobiography* (New York: Bantam Books, 1987), p. 137; Pancho Barnes, quoted in Grover Ted Tate, *The Lady Who Tamed Pegasus: The Story of Pancho Barnes* (Los Angeles: Maverick, 1984), p. 47. Barnes continued: "Whenever she fucked up he would scold her as a child. He kept this up until she almost lost confidence in herself so then he backed off." While few had kind words to say about Putnam personally, Barnes's assessment seems too stark. Many others, including women flyers who knew the couple, found the relationship symbiotic and mutually satisfying.

10 Amelia Earhart, quoted in *New York Times*, March 14, 1937, p. 34; *New York Herald Tribune*, June 21, 1934, p. 1; Fay Gillis Wells at Amelia Earhart Symposium, Smithsonian Institution, reprinted in *Aviation Journal* (June 1983), p. 5.

11 George Palmer Putnam, *Wide Margins: A Publisher's Autobiography* (New York: Harcourt, Brace, 1942), p. 3. The best biographical information about Putnam is found in Lovell, *Sound of Wings*, which presents a very sympathetic assessment of the man and his importance to Earhart.

12 Putnam, *Wide Margins*, p. 252; Lovell, *Sound of Wings*, pp. 83–84.

13 Bradford Washburn, "Amelia Earhart's Last Flight," *Boston Museum of Science Newsletter* 33 (January–February 1984), p. 2.

14 Lovell, *Sound of Wings*, covers Putnam's later career. In all the Hollywood books I have read about the studio system in the 1930s, Putnam is never mentioned; this suggests that he was not a major player.

15 Edward Bernays defined public relations as "(1) information given to the public; (2) persuasion directed at the public to modify attitudes and actions; and (3) efforts to integrate attitudes and actions of an institution with its publics and of publics with that institution." Bernays, *Public Relations* (Norman: University of Oklahoma Press, 1952), p. 3. See also Edward Bernays, *Crystallizing Public Opinion* (New York: Boni and Liveright, 1923); Eric F. Goldman, *Two-Way Street: The Emergence of the Public Relations Counsel* (Boston: Bellman, 1948); and Daniel Boorstin, *The Image* (New York: Atheneum, 1961).
Sometimes Putnam went too far, like his transparent attempt to capitalize on Eleanor Roosevelt's popularity by dubbing Earhart "The First Lady of the Air." (The name did not stick.) Quoted in Lovell, *Sound of Wings*, p. 215. Or his 1935 press release stating, "Amelia Earhart is now a grandmother," when his son David Binney Putnam and wife had a child. Quoted in Rich, *Amelia Earhart*, p. 208.

16   Putnam, *Soaring Wings*, p. 209.

17 Ibid., p. 88; Rich, *Amelia Earhart*, pp. 178, 202. When a researcher does a lot of newspaper research on microfilm, you notice things like this because the Sunday papers take much longer to scan.

18 Amelia Earhart, quoted in *Newsweek*, May 18, 1935, p. 35; George Palmer Putnam, quoted in Rich, *Amelia Earhart*, p. 199; clipping, June 22, 1932, p. 3; Putnam, *Wide Margins*, p. 282.

19 Amelia Earhart, *20 Hrs. 40 Min. Our Flight in the Friendship* (New York: G. P. Putnam's Sons, 1928), pp. 282–83. Hollywood celebrities like Jean Harlow and Carole Lombard often endorsed cigarettes, especially Lucky Strike. For more on smoking in Hollywood, see Cal York, "What Do They Smoke?," *Photoplay* (September 1931). Other products that prominent women endorsed in *Photoplay* included Pond's cream (socialite Anne Morgan), Auburn cars (Marlene Dietrich), and handbags (Carole Lombard and Ginger Rogers).

20 *New York Times*, July 31, 1928, p. 8; Richard Byrd to Amelia Earhart, July 30, 1928, Purdue Special Collections; Earhart, *20 Hrs. 40 Min.*, pp. 282–83; Putnam, *Soaring Wings*, pp. 193–94.

21 A general introduction to endorsements is William M. Freeman, *The Big Name* (New York: Printers' Ink Books, 1957). See also Boorstin, *The Image*.

22 "I would try it again with WASP," the cable which Earhart sent back from Ireland after her flight, was no doubt part of an endorsement deal with the Pratt & Whitney aircraft company. See *Aviation* (July 1932).

23 Similarly, an ad for Stanavo aviation gasoline and engine oil includes a picture taken before the flight along with this text: "Great credit is due Miss Earhart and her associates for the careful preparation contributing to her brilliant flight. Careful preparation had characterized all successful transatlantic flights, the list of which includes every attempt made using Stanavo products." *Aviation* (July 1932).

24 Time Savers were notes, envelopes, and blotters from White and Wyckoff that were "thin-packed to slip into your bag or pocket so you may write while you wait at the restaurant, dressmakers', hairdressers', dentist's, doctor's, between appointments, and on boat, train, or airplane." They had a logo of Amelia Earhart's name, with a red plane and trail cutting across. Sample found in Amelia Earhart Papers, Schlesinger Library, Harvard University.

25 Rich, *Amelia Earhart*, p. 238.

26 Amy Otis Earhart manuscript, undated, Amy Otis Earhart Papers, Schlesinger Library, Harvard University (hereafter AOE Papers); press release, undated, found in American Institute of Aeronautics and Astronautics Collection, Library of Congress.

27 Advertisement, ca. 1933, found in AOE Papers.

28 Sigrid Arne, "Midstream with Modern Women," *Knickerbocker Press*, May 16, 1934, p. 7; "Amelia Earhart Turns from Flying to Designing" (1934), promotional brochure put out by the United States Rubber Company, found in Purdue Special Collections.

29 U.S. Rubber brochure, Purdue Special Collections; Janet Mabie, "A Bird's Eye View of Fashion," *Christian Science Monitor Magazine*, February 7, 1934, p. 3. Or, as Earhart said on another occasion, "Aviation itself is, it seems to me, a great untapped source for fashion inspiration. . . . I am using this type of decorative detail both because it gives a fresh touch to sports clothes and because through it perhaps can bring some of the beauty I have found in aviation closer to all women." U.S. Rubber brochure, Purdue Special Collections.

30 Amy Otis Earhart manuscript; *Women's Wear Daily*, December 11, 1933, p. 19, and *New York Times*, November 24, 1933, p. 30; "Photoplay Announces Macy's Cinema Shop," *Photoplay* (June 1934). A Macy's executive said thirty stores had accepted the franchise: "The idea behind the whole thing is to prevent pirating or reproduction. There is to be no attempt for volume." Quoted in *Women's Wear Daily*, December 11, 1933, p. 19.

31 An article in *Woman's Home Companion* 61 (August 1934), p. 33, also advertised Amelia Earhart patterns for the fashions, available for 25 cents from the Woman's Home Companion Service Bureau.

32 U.S. Rubber brochure, Purdue Special Collections.

33 Putnam, *Soaring Wings*, p. 202; Rich, *Amelia Earhart*, p. 146; clippings found in Purdue Special Collections and Amelia Earhart General File, National Air and Space Museum Archives; *New York Times*, May 16, 1931, p. 19; "Miss Earhart's Adventure on the Floor of the Sea," *Cosmopolitan* (November 1929); *New York Times*, July 23, 1929, p. 18, and July 24, 1929, p. 3. Earhart was upset at the headline MISS EARHART BALKS, which implied she had lost her nerve. In fact, the suit she was wearing was too large and leaked.

34 George Palmer Putnam to President Edward Elliott, June 10, 1935, Purdue Special Collections.

35 Amelia Earhart, "A Friendly Flight across the Country," *New York Times Magazine*, July 9, 1931, pp. 7, 23.

36 Louella Parsons rumor cited in Rich, *Amelia Earhart*, p. 159. Here is the full quote: "Some day, if it's a proper story—if they let me play my unromantic self, slacks, engine grease and all. If something comes along that will be useful in advancing women—if it will help flying—if-if-if-." Quoted in Putnam, *Soaring Wings*, pp. 165–66.

37 Mortimer Franklin, "Amelia Earhart Looks at the Films!," *Screenland* (June 1933), p. 76. She had definite ideas about aviation and Hollywood: "I think it's too bad when aviation movies depend for their excitement upon plane wrecks, lost flyers, and all that sort of thing. Perhaps that's good drama, perhaps it isn't; but it certainly isn't modern aviation. . . . Aviation has grown up, you know. It isn't a plaything anymore. It has become a serious and useful industry." She also spoke out against war. "As an individual I'm opposed to war, anyway, and naturally I think it's extremely unfortunate that war should be emphasized, and to some extent even glorified, in any kind of film." Ibid., p. 29.

38 Mark Lankin, "What Happens to Fan Mail?," *Photoplay* (August 1928), pp. 38–40.

39 Earhart, *20 Hrs. 40 Min.*, p. 281.

40 Quoted in Putnam, *Soaring Wings*, pp. 85, 210.

41 Ibid., p. 86; Amelia Earhart to Harry Manning, February 19, 1934, quoted in Shirley Dobson Gilroy, *Amelia: Pilot in Pearls* (McLean, VA: Link Press, 1985), p. 68. It remains true, however, that there really are not that many personal letters from Earhart extant. In part this is because many of her personal effects were burned in the fire at the Rye house in late 1934. Also her lifestyle was fairly peripatetic, so she was unlikely to save material when she was on the road. (There are no thorough correspondence files for George Putnam either.) The most extensive letters are those to her mother and sister excerpted in Jean L. Backus, ed., *Letters from Amelia, 1901–1937* (Boston: Beacon Press, 1982), drawn from the collections at the Schlesinger Library.

42 After she lent Muriel money to purchase a house, she expected it to be a businesslike relationship: "I'm no scrooge to ask that some acknowledgement of a twenty-five hundred dollar loan be given me. I work hard for my money. Whether or not I shall exact repayment is my business nevertheless Pidge should feel some responsibility for protecting me against the loss of that sum." When she got involved in the summer vacation for the Morrissey family and Mrs. Earhart, she told them where to go and what kind of place to stay in: a nice rental, "not a cheap hole where there are things to put up with. For instance, i do not want you and pidge to do housework. in fact i forbid that." Amelia Earhart to Mrs. Eho, April 27, 1931, and Amelia Earhart to Mother, June 25, 1931, AOE Papers.

43 Amelia Earhart to Manny, December 26, 1928, and Amelia Earhart to Mother, June 2, 1935, AOE Papers.

44 Amelia Earhart to Maw, September 18, 1932, and Amelia Earhart to Mother, December 1, 1931, AOE Papers.

45 Roxana Robinson, *Georgia O'Keeffe: A Life* (New York: Harper & Row, 1989), p. 270.

46 See, for example, George Palmer Putnam to Amy Otis Earhart, November 26, 1935, AOE Papers, in which Putnam tries to explain why Earhart may not be available for some family function. "I guess we will have to leave the decision in all this up to Amelia. For self-protection she simply has to be hard-boiled about getting away from people. Realize, please, this is a problem repeated two or three times a day every day for the last few months."

47 Amelia Earhart, *The Fun of It: Random Records of My Own Flying and of Women in Aviation* (New York: Harcourt, Brace, 1932), p. 87; Putnam, *Soaring Wings*, p. 174.

48 *The Lantern* (July–August 1928), cited in Lovell, *Sound of Wings*, p. 111; Amelia Earhart, "What Miss Earhart Thinks When She's Flying," *Cosmopolitan* (December 1928), p. 28; Earhart, *20 Hrs. 40 Min.*, p. 280.

49 *New York Times*, August 30, 1928, p. 2.

50 Earhart, *The Fun of It*, pp. 209–18. The Schlesinger Library has a copy of the 78 rpm record, which is about two minutes long.

51 For example, see *New York Times Book Review*, September 16, 1928, p. 10; *Saturday Review of Literature*, October 13, 1928, p. 240; *Books*, June 19, 1932, p. 5; *New York Times Book Review*, June 26, 1932, p. 8.

52 Muriel Earhart Morrissey and Carol L. Osborne, *Amelia, My Courageous Sister* (Santa Clara, CA: Osborne, 1987), p. 101; Amelia Earhart and George Palmer Putnam, "My Husband/My Wife," *Redbook* (October 1932), pp. 22–23; Amelia Earhart, "Flying and Fly-Fishing," *Outdoor Life* 62 (December 1934), pp. 16–17; Amelia Earhart, "My Flight from Hawaii," *National Geographic* 65 (May 1935), pp. 593–609.

53 The *New York Times* had the rights to the 1928 and 1932 flights. The *New York Herald Tribune* syndicate paid for exclusive rights to her California–Mexico and Mexico–Newark flights as well as the round-the-world flight. The rights to the 1935 Hawaii–Oakland solo went to the North American Newspaper Alliance, Inc.

54 *New York Herald Tribune*, May 9, 1935, p. 1. Ditto when she flew from Hawaii to California; the *Los Angeles Times*, January 13, 1935, p. 1, noted that she went directly into the Hotel Oakland, where she met with her husband's business representatives and wrote her exclusive story for the *Los Angeles Times* and other papers in the syndicate.

55 Telegram to Amy Otis Earhart inviting her to attend, June 18, 1932, AOE Papers; *New York Times*, July 4, 1928, p. 3, and July 12, 1928, p. 9; *National Geographic* (September 1932), p. 36; Rich, *Amelia Earhart*, p. 161; *New York Times*, December 1, 1928, p. 36; clipping, "Today on the Radio," May 26, 1933, in AOE Papers; Rich, *Amelia Earhart*, p. 208.

56 Putnam, *Soaring Wings*, p. 79; telegram from Amelia Earhart to George Palmer Putnam, April 18, 1936, Purdue Special Collections.

57 Amelia Earhart to Mother, September 6, 1932, and George Palmer Putnam to Mrs. Earhart, September 21, 1935, AOE Papers; Earhart, *20 Hrs. 40 Min.*, p. 281; Amelia Earhart to Amy Otis Earhart, no date, and Amelia Earhart to Mother, January 18, 1936, AOE Papers.

58 Backus, *Letters from Amelia*, p. 149; Rich, *Amelia Earhart*, p. 210; Amelia Earhart itinerary found in AOE Papers. This was just one of several such trips that year. The schedule is truly mind-boggling, especially when one realizes that she was doing a fair bit of it by car.

59 On fees, see Lovell, *Sound of Wings*, p. 205, and Rich, *Amelia Earhart*, p. 159. At $300 a shot, that represents $40,000 in income a year.

60 Amy Otis Earhart manuscript, no date, AOE Papers; Rich, *Amelia Earhart*, p. 219.

61 George Palmer Putnam to F. C. Crawford, November 30, 1935, Purdue Special Collections; Amelia Earhart to Mother, March 8, 1935, and November 3, 1935, in AOE Papers; Amelia Earhart to Hiram Bingham, July 19, 1932, Amelia Earhart General File, National Air and Space Museum Archives; Amelia Earhart to Mother, February 14, 1933, AOE Papers.

62 "The Reminiscences of Muriel Earhart Morrissey" (1960), Oral History Collection, Columbia University, p. 11; Fay Gillis Wells at Amelia Earhart Symposium, Smithsonian Institution, reprinted in *Aviation Journal* (May 1983), p. 5.

63 Address to DAR, April 21, 1933, found in Muriel Earhart Morrissey Papers, Schlesinger Library, Harvard University.

64 Mary Spencer to Amy Otis Earhart, March 15, 1935, and Harriet Palmer to Amy Otis Earhart, August 10, 1941, AOE Papers; Alice Kalousdian, quoted in Gilroy, *Amelia: Pilot in Pearls*, p. 50; Jane Dow Bromberg, December 19, 1984, quoted in Rich, *Amelia Earhart*, p. 82.

1. Jake Coolidge, Amelia Earhart, from the "Lady Lindy" series, June 1928

"All the News That's Fit to Print."

The New York Times.

Copyright, 1928, by The New York Times Company.

THE WEATHER
Rain today and tomorrow; not much change in temperature.
Temperature yesterday—Max. 72, min. 57.
For weather report see Page 42.

VOL. LXXVII....No. 25,699. • • • NEW YORK, MONDAY, JUNE 4, 1928. TWO CENTS In Greater New York | THREE CENTS Within 200 Miles | FOUR CENTS Elsewhere in the U. S.

BOSTON GIRL STARTS FOR ATLANTIC HOP, REACHES HALIFAX, MAY GO ON TODAY; AUSTRALIANS FLYING ON TOWARD FIJI

PEKING UNHARMED AS NORTHERN HOSTS POUR OUT OF CITY

Iron Discipline Averts Looting by Troops, but Government Strips Its Buildings.

CIVILIANS IN WILD FLIGHT

Mukden Refugees Jam Station Under Broiling Sun and Ride Away on the Tops of Cars.

CHANG'S TRAIN IS BOMBED

War Lord, Slightly Hurt, Reaches Mukden—Many Others Killed and Wounded—Southerners Blamed.

By HALLETT ABEND.

Special Cable to THE NEW YORK TIMES.

PEKING, June 3.—Thanks to iron discipline, the evacuation of Peking by Marshal Chang Tso-lin's troops is proceeding without incidents or looting, though the Dictator himself departed at 1:15 o'clock this morning on one of four special trains which carried the entire Government, except the Ministers of the Interior and Foreign Affairs, who remained, one to help preserve order and the other to maintain contact with foreign Governments.

Twelve hours after Chang's departure the main railway station of Peking, broiling under the June sun, was witnessing with amazement the continued orderly evacuation of the major portion of the undefeated Ankuochun army, 165,000 strong, and so far not a shot has been fired within hearing of the Northern capital.

Civilian Fugitives in Wild Scramble.

In contrast to the orderly military evacuation, the flight of the civilian adherents of the Ankuochun [Northern military alliance] was marked by the wildest confusion. On the platform of the station, amid an odd medley of carriages, horses and household effects, men, women and children were sleeping prone upon the concrete flooring, despite the heat and swarms of flies.

Every train is carrying people on the roofs of the coaches exposed to the broiling sun. Some are taking the trip in their own automobiles loaded on flat cars surrounded by potted palms and oleanders.

Though there has been no looting by the soldiery or civilians, the retiring Government has been stripping the Government buildings. Even the Bureau of Printing and Engraving, the only plant in China that has printed good paper money, has been denuded of machinery, and the whole staff, exceeding a thousand employes, has been moved to Mukden on a special train with a promise of more pay.

Chang Forms Alliance for Return.

Foreigners are not yet apprehensive, but a growing tension and uneasiness are visible among the Chinese over the possibilities of the next forty-eight hours. Peking's million people, at present without an actual government, are uncertain when the Nationalists will arrive to take charge.

Chang Tso-lin's farewell message, broadcast to all Provinces, hints at his possible return. He does not surrender his title of dictator but merely moves over to Manchuria to avoid further bloodshed and the possibility of further foreign entanglements.

At a farewell conference of Marshal Chang Tso-lin, General Sun Chuan-fang, Commander of the Shantung Army, and Chang Tsung-chang, the Military Governor of Shantung, who has also been in the field, the last named officer took full blame for the debacle of the Northern armies. Then the three leaders pledged an alliance of "all for one and one for all" until conditions were propitious to attempt to retake Peking and extend their sway over all China.

Anxious Wait for Nationalists.

With the bodily removal of the entire Ankuochun Government, Peking is awaiting with anxiety the arrival of the Nationalists. All Northern taxes have been suspended automatically and future business rests on the knees of the gods.

Chang Tso-lin was accompanied in the exodus by a large number of conservative civilians who feared semi-Communist taxation and radical labor agitation, stirring the masses to the point of an attack upon capitalists.

Since midnight the military evacuation has been proceeding at an accelerated pace, not only by rail, but also by motor trucks, pack animals, donkey carts and camel caravans, which are taking the newly repaired highway via Nanow Pass, through Jehol to Mukden.

All of the legation guards are on their toes for any emergency. Most of the foreigners living in the Tartar city and the Chinese city have their trunks and bags packed and ready to start for the shelter of the legation quarter walls if disturbances begin.

Flagless Capital Calmly Expectant.

PEKING, June 3 (AP).—No flag floated over the empty Presidential Palace in Peking today. The five-barred emblem of the North China Republic was pulled down when Chang Tso-lin gave up his two years' dictatorship and left for Mukden early this morning. The expected crop of the sun banners of the vic-

Continued on Page Nine.

Staten Island Trolley Men Strike Today; Company to Halt Service to 20,000 Riders

Service of five Staten Island street car lines will be suspended at noon today when 200 employes of the Richmond Railways, Inc., of Staten Island, walk out on strike as a result of a vote taken early yesterday after the operating company refused the men's demands for an increase in wages of 10 cents an hour.

Edward J. Leahey, President of the Staten Island local union of the American Association of Street and Electric Railway Employes, said that the company had not been notified of the proposed walkout as the men's demands were rejected on Friday and no further action was necessary.

The lines affected are the St. George-Elizabethport Ferry, South Beach, Silver Lake, Bull Head and Manor Road between Midland and South Beaches. About 15,000 commuters and between 5,000 and 6,000 other passengers will be compelled to find some other means of transportation from their homes to the municipal ferry at St. George.

S. H. Firena, General Manager of the company, said last night that no attempt would be made to bring in strike-breakers and the company would simply cease to operate the street cars.

The Tompkins Bus Company, which operates lines of buses on some of the routes affected by the strike, will attempt to take care of some of the commuters and others can be served by the lines of the Staten Island Rapid Transit System.

Mr. Fuina said that commuters, with the exception of those in Port Richmond and Arlington, would not be seriously inconvenienced because buses touched all the points the trolley lines did. The railway company lines on the island serve the north and eastern sections, with a short line through the centre.

The decision to strike was reached at a meeting held in Emerald Hall, New Brighton, by the railway employes. They are now receiving 65 and 70 cents an hour, and ask a flat increase to 80 cents for all employes.

FINDS A 'DEATH RAY' FATAL TO HUMANS

German Scientist Says It Inflames and Destroys Cells, Hence Aids in Disease.

EXPECTS TO SPLIT ATOM

Dr. Graichen Has Device to Make Blind See With Light Sent Through the Skull.

Wireless to THE NEW YORK TIMES.

BERLIN, June 3.—The discovery of a new "death ray," capable of destroying, though not intended to destroy, human life, has just been announced by Dr. Graichen, a young physicist and engineer employed as an experimenter by the Siemens Halske Electric Company.

Dr. Graichen described the effects of his invention as follows:

"Turned on small living creatures my rays caused an inflamation of the cells, which becomes deadly within five or six hours. I have no doubt that the larger animals, and even human beings, would be affected in the same way. Plants when struck by my rays die quickly, generally in less than fifteen minutes."

The scientist has also invented a process for making the sightless see. President Hindenburg wrote him an autograph letter congratulating him on his discovery and expressing the hope that his efforts would ameliorate the condition of the blind.

Speaking about his ray he said:

"The apparatus created by me is not entirely new. I simply found means greatly to strengthen cathode rays by combining the cathode tube with the Roentgen tube, thus producing soft rays in such manner as to lengthen the cathode rays from a few centimeters to six meters and more. This result is not solely accomplished by the use of Roentgen rays, however, but is largely due to the fact that I produce the rays directly, instead of with the aid of heated electrons, as used by the American scientist Coolidge, working along the same lines. My system not only produces primary and secondary cathode rays but also positive ions of enormous velocity."

Regarding the scientific value of his invention, the doctor said:

"From my experiments I am convinced that it will be very useful in combating cancer. In a number of cases I turned the rays on rats infected with cancer and ascertained that the diseased cells were destroyed within a short time. Other experiments proved that bacteria which resist even X-rays die quickly when exposed to my rays. They also have the capability of the fluorescence of gases and change the color of metallic and other solid substances. Glass, for instance, becomes brownish and colorless crystals begin to glow an intensive red. The greatest and most promising possibility of my invention is the breaking up of the atom and the changing of elements. This will be possible as soon as I am able to use a million or more volts. I have already ascertained that my rays separate the positive nucleus of the atom from the electrons circling around it, but the actual splitting of the atom and the changing of the elements will be possible only if the

Continued on Page Ten.

FRANC AT 4 CENTS IS BELIEVED DECIDED

Poincare Is Expected to Stabilize at That Rate Between July 15 and Aug. 15.

MANY WANT HIGHER RATIO

Move to Raise Money's Value Before Fixing It Is Strong, but Likely to Fail.

By EDWIN L. JAMES.

Special Cable to THE NEW YORK TIMES.

PARIS, June 3.—It is believed that the Poincaré Government will stabilize the franc at five paper francs to one gold franc, and that it will take this step not sooner than July 15 nor later than Aug. 15. The question of what the Premier would do with the franc has loomed as the biggest issue in French politics, an issue not only national in its interest but international as well.

Although during the campaign which ended in the elections of May 24 it was generally accepted that a vote for M. Poincaré meant a vote for stabilization, since the favorable result of the elections the Premier has been the target of a strong movement for further revalorization of the franc, a movement which has assumed an importance probably not fully realized outside of France. And the leaders of this movement have known enough to invoke the one argument which would appeal to the exact, legal mind of M. Poincaré, namely, that stabilization now would mean 80 per cent. bankruptcy for the State. This argument has had its appeal in the ears of the Premier.

However, the proponents of stabilization at the present rate of the franc have not been idle and, having back of them the vast majority of financial and business leaders of the country, they have made a defense of their cause which seems due to be victorious. Between the two arguments M. Poincaré has come to see that the real choice lies between the producers and the non-producers of the country.

Producers Want Stabilization.

For it is the producers who wish stabilization at the present rate, while it is the non-producers, who are living from rentes and other investments, who wish the franc to mount further, for they would benefit from the additional burden such a movement would place upon the industry of France.

It would be indeed easy for M. Poincare to place the franc at a higher figure. With his signature he could put the franc at 100 to the pound and twenty to the dollar, instead of the current rate of 125 to the pound and twenty-five to the dollar.

The Treasury and the Bank of France have had to use some $50,000,000 in the past week on the exchange market to prevent the franc from rising. These purchases, largely from abroad, are due in no small part to propagation of a rumor that M. Poincaré had decided to stabilize at 110 to the pound instead of 125.

Not a day passes without stabilizers and revalorizers placing their arguments before the Premier, and

Continued on Page Six.

Egypt Bars Public From Seeing Mummies; Royal Remains to Be Put in a Private Hall

Wireless to THE NEW YORK TIMES.

CAIRO, June 3.—Modern Egypt has awakened to the necessity of preserving the dignity of its ancient Kings, whose mummified remains are no longer to be exposed to the view of curious visitors.

Some time ago a proposal was made by Ismail Sidky Pasha, the well known Liberal leader, to the effect that all mummies of Egyptian Kings should be reinterred in their original tombs and sarcophagi. The proposal did not meet with official approval, but a commission was appointed to study the question.

The chief argument adduced by Sidky Pasha was that there was no scientific object in exposing the mummies, the only justification being the satisfaction of the vulgar curiosity of visitors. He drew a parallel with the memory of Julius Caesar, whose mummy, if discovered by the Italians, he contended would never have been exposed to the public gaze. He further appealed to the conscience of independent Egypt by pointing out that one of the mummies exposed was that of Amasis I, who drove Hyksos from Egypt, thereby restoring the country's independence.

While the arguments appealed to the commissioners, they found the proposal impracticable, owing to the fragile nature of some of the mummies and also because most of the tombs are now unfit to receive the royal remains.

They finally decided that the mummies should be collected in a special hall of the Cairo Museum, which should be accessible only to Egyptologists and visitors of mark, armed with the special authorization of the Minister of Public Works. This ruling will be put into force within a few days' time.

At the same time the tomb in the Valley of the Kings, containing the exposed mummy of Amenophis II, which before the Tut-ankh-Amen discoveries was the chief attraction in the valley, will be closed to the public.

REPUBLICANS FACE CONVENTION BATTLE LIKE THAT OF 1912

Vanguard at Kansas City Finds Shadow There of Split as in Roosevelt's Day.

HOOVER FIGHT A PROBLEM

Farm Revolt Is Not Minimized by Early Arrivals—Smith's Strength Is Disturbing.

DELEGATE CONTESTS TODAY

Smoot, on Scene Preparatory to Drafting Platform, Is Silent on Agrarian Plank.

By W. A. WARN.

Special to The New York Times.

KANSAS CITY, Mo., June 3.—That the Republican National Convention which will open here a week from Tuesday will rival in thrills, interest and importance to the Republican party, the fateful Chicago convention of 1912 is the expectation of practically all of the small advance guard of party leaders who are already beginning to assemble here.

The convention of 1912 carried in its wake Roosevelt led insurgency on such a large scale that it virtually split the party through its middle and kept the Republicans out of the White House for eight long, lean years, and out of control of Congress for six.

The leaders assembled here are not a very cheerful lot, even though there is today no Roosevelt or anyone with his power to attract, who can lead a disgruntled wing out into the wilderness, to divide and cripple their party.

The brewing revolt of farmers in the Corn Belt, following the second veto by President Coolidge of the McNary-Haugen Farm Relief bill, the looming fight over the proposed nomination of Secretary Hoover, and the prospect of the Democrats nominating a candidate with such a demonstrated vote getting potentiality as Governor Smith of New York are possibilities casting before them a broad shadow, bound to affect both the tone and the temper of the convention.

"Stop Hoover" Cry Raised.

With very many of the party leaders already on the scene or expected for tomorrow's meeting of the Republican National Committee to hear and sit in judgment of contests the dominant thought is "stop Hoover." They will be burning midnight oil from now until nominations have become the order of business in the convention over strategic moves to accomplish that purpose.

Again, another batch of leaders will spend long hours at night pondering plans to "put Hoover over," which, with the setbacks suffered through recent primary defeats in Indiana and West Virginia by the Secretary and the protest against his nomination from the agrarian States, which has not yet materialized but is expected, will not be the easy job Mr. Hoover's supporters would like to have it appear, unless all early signs fail.

The "Draft Coolidge" brigade apparently is quite determined to project the President's name into the turmoil which will begin with balloting at the convention. Nothing but a new and more unequivocal demurrer than any that has come from Mr. Coolidge as yet will stop that.

Coolidge Ultimatum Expected.

While no one now on the ground is in a position to speak for the President, there is an uneasy feeling even among those fathering the project that such a protest will be forthcoming at a time considered proper by the President for delivering his ultimatum.

In this connection it is regarded as significant that the Administration will be very strongly represented at the convention. One member of the President's Cabinet, Secretary Hubert Work of the Interior Department, is already here, directing activities at Secretary Hoover's convention headquarters, of which there are several maintained by separate groups of Hoover supporters. Secretary Mellon will be at the convention, as head of the Pennsylvania delegation. Secretary of Agriculture Jardine, Postmaster General New, Secretary of War Davis, and Secretary Davis of the Department of Labor are other Cabinet members expected.

Today word was received that Everett Sanders, secretary to the President, will attend the convention, whether as a visitor or as an official observer it is not known.

While the latest estimates from the Hoover headquarters place the prospective strength of Secretary Hoover at 531 votes in the convention, leaders not allied with the Hoover forces who have looked the field of delegates over, today firmly insisted that his strength does not exceed 425.

There will be 1,089 delegates in the convention, and 545 votes will be necessary to nominate. Some seventy-three Hoover delegates are involved in contests to be decided by the Republican National Committee, the hearings to begin tomorrow.

Farm Revolt Called Serious.

Leaders who have arrived here from the East were making anxious inquiries of Republic National Committeemen from Western States to

Continued on Page Four.

FOUR LEFT KAUAI AT DAWN

Whole Population Out to Wave Godspeed to Crew of Southern Cross.

NEARING 1,400-MILE MARK

Ten Hours Out Fliers Report Motor Trouble 'OK' a Little Later, Then More Spitting.

TWO ISLES IN 3,180 MILES

Hazardous Hop From Hawaii Is Longest Over-Water Flight Ever Attempted.

Plane Is 1,378 Miles Out From Hawaii in 13 Hours

By The Associated Press.

SAN FRANCISCO, June 3.—The Southern Cross has made an average of more than 90 knots since leaving the Barking Sands, on the Isle of Kauai, for Suva, Fiji, this morning, said a message received from the plane by the naval radio station here at 9:20 P. M. (6:50 P. M. Honolulu Time and 1:20 A. M. Monday New York Daylight-Saving Time). The message follows:

"6 P. M. (evidently Honolulu Time)—Have made good 1,225 [nautical miles, about 1,378 land miles], giving an average of over 90 knots. Altitude 2,500 feet now. Lots better up here and much cooler."

[The Southern Cross took off at 5:20 A. M. Honolulu Time. Thus she was about 12 hours and 40 minutes out when this report was sent.]

By VERN HINKLEY.

Wireless to THE NEW YORK TIMES.

HONOLULU, June 3.—The monoplane Southern Cross, bound from Oakland, Cal., to Melbourne, Australia, hopped off from the Island of Kauai at 5:20 o'clock this morning (11:50 A. M. New York Daylight Saving Time) on the second long leg of its transpacific flight, the objective being Suva, Fiji, 3,180 miles away.

If Captain Charles Kingsford-Smith, pilot and commander, and his three companions, Captain Charles T. P. Ulm, co-pilot; Captain Harry Lyon, navigator, and Charles Warren, radio man, are able to maintain the pace they set during the first six hours of their flight from the Barking Sands at Kauai they should land at Suva in about thirty-two hours, that is about 8 o'clock tomorrow night, New York Time.

The take-off was as commonplace as though the airmen were passengers boarding a train.

"It is beautiful weather for our work," Captain Kingsford-Smith remarked, gazing for a moment at the full moon low on the western horizon just before he climbed into the cockpit.

The motors were warmed up for ten minutes, the blocks were pulled from in front of the wheels and the Southern Cross then sped down the runway, climbing into the air in less than 2,500 feet and disappearing into the dim morning sky to the south.

Averaging 100 Miles an Hour.

A position report received here at 11 A. M., Honolulu time (5:30 P. M. New York Daylight Saving Time), indicated that they were then about 600 miles on their way and making a speed of about 100 miles an hour.

Provided the gasoline consumption does not exceed that on the Oakland-Wheeler Field leg, which the fliers completed on Friday, they will reach their goal at Suva with fuel enough

Continued on Page Three.

Times Wide World Photos.

GIRL WHO IS TO BRAVE AN ATLANTIC FLIGHT.
Two Poses of Miss Amelia Earhart of Boston, Who Flew Yesterday on The First Lap of an Air Trip to England.

WOMAN TO BE CO-PILOT

Miss Earhart, Social Worker and Flier, to Aid Wilmer Stultz.

TAKE OFF AT BOSTON HARBOR

Three-Motored Fokker Plane Friendship, Sold by Byrd, Fitted With Pontoons.

RADIO CAN SEND AND HEAR

Plans, Backed by Mechanical Science Corporation, Kept Silent for Seven Weeks.

Special to The New York Times.

BOSTON, June 3.—At one minute after 6:30 this morning the tri-motored Fokker monoplane Friendship rose from the waters of Boston Harbor and headed eastward into the beams of the rising sun. Her destination is England, after a stop-over for refuelling at Trepassey, N. F.

This evening, however, word came back from Halifax that Wilmer Stultz, the pilot, had landed the plane there, after encountering dense fog along the Nova Scotia coast. With predictions for clearing weather around Newfoundland tomorrow, he expects to be able to get over to Trepassey, a matter of five hours' flying, possibly early enough to fuel up and start off on the actual Atlantic flight tomorrow afternoon.

Woman a Co-Pilot.

On board the Friendship is an American girl, eager to be the first of her sex actually to cross the Atlantic by air. She is Amelia Earhart of Boston, amateur aviatrix and professional social worker. Miss Earhart has owned her own plane and is credited with 500 or more "solo" hours in the air. In the present flight she is known to have substantial backing from friends.

During the present transatlantic flight Miss Earhart will take her turn at the controls, but the pilot in charge is Stultz, who has a distinguished record as a "big-ship" man, navigator and all-around air expert. His flying mechanic is Louis Edward Gordon of Texas, better known as "Slim."

Secrecy has surrounded the flight's entire preparation, covering some seven weeks, and was successfully maintained until today. This was largely accomplished because the big Fokker, officially recorded as NX-4204, was originally purchased by Commander Richard E. Byrd for use on his forthcoming Antarctic expedition. Some time ago Byrd, revising his equipment plans, sold the plane. Announcement of the sale was not made until last Friday. Meantime, the preparation of the plane at Boston had been accepted as experimental work for Commander Byrd.

Plane Equipped With Pontoons.

Of primary technical interest has been the equipment of the plane with specially designed pontoons. This is the first time an American three-engined plane has had this equipment, or that one has been so outfitted for transoceanic flights. Commander Byrd himself maintains that a three-motor ship, with pontoons, is the ideal craft for long over-water work.

The present ownership of the Fokker is somewhat shrouded in mystery. Officially it is the property of the Mechanical Science Corporation. For the corporation, George Palmer Putnam, New York publisher and explorer, is announced as spokesman. The work of technical preparation for the flight has been in charge of Commander Robert E. P. Elmer, U. S. N., retired.

Take Off in Early Morning.

In Boston harbor this morning only about a dozen people witnessed the take-off. At 4:45 A. M. they gathered on Boston's famous T-Dock and thence embarked on the tugboat Sadie Ross. Stultz, Miss Earhart and Gordon were promptly put on board the plane, moored just off the Jeffrey Yacht Club in East Boston. On the tug were Mr. Putnam, Commander Elmer, Mrs. Stultz and a few friends, the latter including Miss Marian Perkins, head of Boston's noted settlement centre, Denison House, with which Miss Earhart is associated as a director and a worker.

Neither reporters nor newspaper photographers were present. The only cameramen on hand were J. E. Coolidge, local representative of Paramount News, with his assistants.

Soon after 5 o'clock, "Slim" Gor-

POLAR HUNTER JOINS ITALIA RELIEF SHIP

Man Who Knows Every Mountain in Spitsbergen Islands Goes With the Hobby.

HOLM PLANS FLIGHT SOON

Russian Radio Amateur Reports Nobile S O S Message From Franz Josef Land.

By FREDERIK RAMM.

Wireless to THE NEW YORK TIMES.

OSLO, Norway, June 3.—The Braganza, which left Kings Bay last night with thirteen Italians and Norwegian hunters as leaders of an expedition to seek the Italia, intends to force its way to the north coast of Spitsbergen in the hope of reaching Reindeer Land, a big flat peninsula at the entrance to Wijde Bay, where it is possible that the airship struck one of the big mountains of the region.

The weather was fine for the first time since the Italia started on its last flight. The Braganza has a wireless installed and, according to its published plans, will stay on the north coast eight days.

Early this morning the Hobby arrived at Advent Bay, its belated arrival being due to rough weather. The Hobby stayed only a few hours to take on board dog-team sledges and the polar-bear hunter, Hilmar Nois, who has lived in Spitsbergen for nine years.

M. Nois knows every bay, glacier and mountain in the whole archipelago and his leadership for sledge expeditions is highly valued. Immediately after loading the Hobby left Advent Bay for Kings Bay, where it will arrive early tomorrow morning.

In case of good weather Lieutenant Luetzow Holm will make the trip northward by plane for the first reconnoissance.

There is no news from the Ingerfire with Captain Reiser-Larsen and his plane aboard, but it will probably

Continued on Page Three.

FOG FORCES STULTZ TO STAY AT HALIFAX

Friendship Starts Again After Stopping in Harbor There, but Puts Back.

HOP TO TREPASSEY TODAY

Pilot Describes How He Flew Through Hole in the Mist to Perfect Landing.

Special to The New York Times.

HALIFAX, N. S., June 3.—Out of the fog that hung thick along the coast of Nova Scotia, a three-motored Fokker monoplane dropped down to a mooring near the Halifax Naval Air Station at 11 o'clock this morning. The plane was the Friendship en route to London, piloted by Wilmer Stultz and carrying as other members of the crew Miss Amelia Earhart of Boston and Lou Gordon, flight mechanic.

After remaining a while on the placid waters of the Passage, the pontoon-equipped ship took the air again, the fog having lifted. She headed out to sea, but thirty minutes later was back at the station again. Off shore she had once more run into heavy fog banks, according to air station officials, and her pilot had decided to postpone any further attempt for the day.

Makes Perfect Landing.

Stultz reported that he had taken off from Boston Harbor about 6:30 o'clock. Aside from increasing fog as he approached Halifax, the voyage was uneventful, the plane performing perfectly. Stultz said that he passed probably fifty miles beyond Halifax before the persistent fog caused him to turn back.

In a temporary rift he found the harbor at Halifax and made a perfect landing. According to local airmen the success of this forced landing gave a fine demonstration of the effectiveness of pontoon equipment for airplanes for long over-water flights. With wheels, a ship in the fog must keep on blindly or retreat to the nearest known landing field. But with pontoons, "any place that is wet," as Stultz says, is a ready-made landing field.

Hop to Trepassey Today.

Tonight the weather forecast gives fair weather with westerly winds for tomorrow and at the air station it was said that the plane would probably take the air early tomorrow morning for Trepassey. It is understood that the Friendship will re-fuel at Trepassey and thence undertake the Atlantic crossing. Her destination is said to be London.

Air station officials said that they heard a big plane droning in the thick fog about 2,000 feet up during the morning. A Canadian seaplane was due here today from Ottawa and the officials thought that this was the ship they heard. But a few minutes later, out of the narrow rift in the fog, Stultz and his crew

Continued on Page Two.

I. R. T. Scrubs and Paints in Clean-Up Week; Elevated Cars Will Be a Brighter Yellow

The Interborough Rapid Transit Company is observing clean-up week at the instance of the Transit Commission. An extra force of men is at work, washing windows, scrubbing floors and seats and in some instances painting cars long without paint.

The commission has ordered the company to polish up its equipment, and more than 200 cars were put in shape last week. The workmen have been particularly directed to scrape and scrub off the ceilings of the cars and repaint them the glossy white which they were originally, but which long since has been covered with grime.

The commission's order also includes the elevated cars. These cars are receiving a new coat of light orange, a shade lighter than the elevated cars were when the orange was first applied. Fifty-eight elevated cars have been so treated and some of the refurbished rolling stock will be seen this week.

The Transit Commission recently directed its force of inspectors to survey the Interborough equipment. Officials of the company were called into conference and the reports of the inspectors showing most of the car interiors to be dirty were laid before them.

As a result of the conferences the company agreed to clean up the cars and repaint those needing it. Transit Commission inspectors are supervising the work and reporting to the commission. A total of 1,299 elevated cars are to be repainted outside and cleaned and revarnished inside.

2. "Boston Girl Starts for Atlantic Hop," *New York Times*, June 4, 1928

3. Jake Coolidge, Amelia Earhart, from the "Lady Lindy" series, June 1928

4. Unidentified Photographer, Amelia Earhart, Wilmer Stultz, and Lou Gordon, early June 1928

5. *New York Times*, June 10, 1928

Sunday,
June 10, 1928

The New York Times

Rotogravure
Picture Section
In Two Parts

6

NORWAY STARTS THE CHEERING FOR A NEW HERO OF THE AIR BEFORE
THE REST OF THE WORLD HAS A CHANCE: SIR GEORGE WILKINS
and His Companion on His Arctic Flight, Lieutenant Carl Ben Eielson, Arrive in Oslo.
(© P. & A.)

"LADY LINDY" READY FOR HER FLIGHT: MISS
AMELIA EARHART,
Who in Her Flying Costume Resembles the Most Famous
Aviator of All, as She Appeared Before the Start From
Boston to Fly Across to England.
(Times Wide World Photos.)

A MEET-
ING OF TWO
ARCTIC COMMUTERS: SIR GEORGE WILKINS
Visits Captain Roald Amundsen, Who Preceded Him Over
the Top of the World, at the Explorer's House Near Oslo.
(Times Wide World Photos.)

A FIRST-CLASS PASSENGER COMES ABOARD: SIR GEORGE
WILKINS'S PLANE,
in Which He Flew From Alaska to Spitsbergen, Loaded on a Steamer at
Tromsoe, in Northern Norway, for Shipment to the South.
(Times Wide World Photos.)

THE CREW OF THE FRIENDSHIP IN BOSTON: MISS AMELIA
EARHART
With Wilmer Stultz, the co-Pilot, and Lou Gordon, the Mechanician, Be-
fore the Start of the Friendship for Newfoundland.
(Paramount News-Associated Press.)

THE START OF THE FRIENDSHIP'S FLIGHT TO THE NORTH: MISS
AMELIA EARHART'S PLANE,
Which Is Almost a Duplicate of the One Used by Commander Byrd in His
Crossing Last Year, Heading Out of Boston Harbor.
(Times Wide World Photos, Boston Bureau.)

FIREWORKS ON A RACE COURSE: FRITZ VON OPEL
Giving the First Public Demonstration of His Rocket Car, Which Reached a Speed of 100 Kilometers an Hour Within Two Seconds of the Start and Later
Touched 250 on the Track of the Avus Speedway in Berlin.
(Times Wide World Photos, Berlin Bureau.)

Sunday,
July 1, 1928

The New York Times

Rotogravure
Picture Section
In Two Parts

7

A PASSENGER FROM AMERICA LANDS AT SOUTHAMPTON:
MISS AMELIA EARHART,
First Woman to Fly Across the Atlantic, Looking Out of the
Door of the Friendship as the Plane Taxis to a Landing
on Its Arrival From Burry Point in South Wales.
(Times Wide World Photos.)

A BOSTON SETTLEMENT WORKER FLIES INTO FAME: MISS AMELIA EARHART and Her Two Companions, Wilmer Stultz and Lou Gordon, Mobbed by a Crowd of Admirers on Their Arrival at Southampton From Burry Point. (Times Wide World Photos.)

THE FIRST PHOTOGRAPH TAKEN FROM AN AIR-
PLANE ON THE ATLANTIC CROSSING:
THE AMERICA
as She Was Seen From the Friendship 70 Miles Off the
Coast of Ireland. The Picture Was Taken by Miss Earhart
Through a Door in the Bottom of the Airplane.
(Times Wide World Photos.)

WHEN THE DAWN CAME UP OVER THE ATLANTIC: CLOUD BANKS ABOVE THE WATER
as the Crew of the Friendship First Saw the Light of a New Day on Their Way Across the Ocean.
(Times Wide World Photos.)

THE CHANGES LONDON MADE IN A FAMOUS
AVIATOR: MISS AMELIA EARHART,
Who Arrived in Her Flying Suit and Helmet, Appears
for the First of the Celebrations in Her Honor
Dressed in "Mufti."
(Times Wide World Photos.)

6. *New York Times*, July 1, 1928

7. Unidentified Photographer, Amelia Earhart in her Ascot gown at the home of Amy Guest, late June 1928

THE CAMERA, TOO, HANDED US BRICKBATS—THESE ARE CULLED FROM OUR LESS (OH, FAR!) FLATTERING PHOTOGRAPHIC SOUVENIRS

8. Page from Amelia Earhart's *20 Hrs. 40 Min.*, showing Earhart, Wilmer Stultz, and Lou Gordon, 1928

9. Unidentified Photographer. Amelia Earhart with a bouquet presented to her at the Boston airport, July 1928

10. Unidentified Photographer. Amelia Earhart, 1930

11. Amelia Earhart, "What Miss Earhart Thinks When She's Flying," *Cosmopolitan*, December 1928

12. Amelia Earhart, "Try Flying Yourself," *Cosmopolitan*, November 1928

What MISS EARHART

An Intimate Article Written While

She Was Vagabonding by Air

VAGABONDING means change. One of its greatest charms is the excitement of moving from place to place, meeting new people, encountering unexpected situations. Whatever the means of travel—hobos usually aren't particular—the effect is the same.

One may tramp afoot, horseback it, or pilgrimage modernly by automobile. Most of America seems to elect the last-named method, at least in that wide segment of the continent which I have looked down upon this autumn. The white and gray ribbons that are roads everywhere are pockmarked with cars, appearing from the air like flat-topped beetles crawling so slowly across the landscape. (That lack of speed, as viewed from aloft, is remarkable; even swift railroad-trains seem sluggish.)

As I write this I am a hobo of the air, sojourning briefly in a tiny town of western Texas, midway—and more—on a transcontinental venture in aviation vagabondage. A hobo of sorts, and enjoying it hugely.

This for me is vacation, a relaxation from writers' cramp, if you will. For my first flight across the Atlantic in the Friendship was followed by my first book. The latter concerned the former. The hop, I think, was rather easier than the writing. At least crossing the Atlantic consumed only "20 hrs. and 40 min." (which I used for the title of the book), while the manuscript required a strenuous month and more.

With authorship behind, I took to the air. The journey started from a polo field at Rye, casually enough. As a matter of fact, there are many pilots today, flying for sport alone, who hop about the country as they choose. In some ways that sort of air touring is no more arduous than a long train or automobile journey, especially if undertaken in leisurely fashion.

The extent of my own air vagabondage developed as I flew westward in my little sport biplane, the one, by the way, in which Lady Heath "soloed" from London to Cape Town and back. It seemed to me an entertaining addition to the little Avian's record to add America's continental crossing to its end-to-ending of Africa.

The first stage of the journey took me to Pittsburgh, Dayton, Terre Haute, St. Louis, Muskogee, and on into New Mexico. After straying from the course, I finally landed at Pecos, Texas, 187 miles from El Paso. And there I stayed for several days writing this for Cosmopolitan and waiting while parts of a misbehaving motor were repaired at El Paso and returned to me at Pecos.

In this cross-country flying I have learned from experience something of the difficulties which daily face air-mail pilots, and those who have to fly, on schedule, routes across country.

Automobilists universally complain about the lack of parking space. For the cars of the air the dearth of parking space—that is to say, landing-fields—is even more serious. When a plane's motor is disabled the pilot must make a landing. True, the machine can be controlled in the air and glide gently down, but it must have a smooth open space for alighting.

As there is always the possibility of some failure in anything man-made, so even with well-behaved motors today occasional descents are inevitable. And when they come, "parking space" is essential—often a matter of life-saving. The field need not be elaborate, although naturally the pilot turns with delight to the air-port offering hangar service and complete equipment. But where air travel does not warrant great expenditures, after all only a smooth marked space is needed.

It is sometimes wise for a plane to stop for some minor adjustment which the pilot cannot make in the air. The automobile on the highroad, if the engine knocks or the brake band binds, can halt at a garage. But in the air there are no garages. The pilot must find a place to come down safely if he is to avoid serious trouble later.

And oh, for a country-wide campaign of sign-painting! Every community abreast of the times should have a display in large white or chrome yellow letters painted on some flat roof announcing its name to the world which flies. An arrow pointing the direction to the nearest landing-field is also desirable.

Imagine automobiling without signs! Imagine trying to recognize a town the way fliers do—a hundred-mile-an-hour look at a checker-board of streets and roofs, trees and fields, with highways and railroads radiating and crisscrossing and perhaps a river or two to complicate—or simplify—the geography lesson.

The transcontinental air derby of this autumn focused fresh interest upon the importance of naming towns. All the places selected for control stops—that is, official "station-stops" on the route—were compelled to paint both the name of the town and directional arrows for guidance from aloft. This air honor-roll included New York, Harrisburg, McKeesport, Columbus, Terre Haute, St. Louis, Kansas City, Wichita, Oklahoma City, Fort Worth, Abilene, Midland, Pecos, El Paso, Lordsburg, Tucson, Yuma and Los Angeles.

On my own transcontinental air-gipsying, I saw few towns properly named until California was reached. Some of the community "sign-boards" had been so neglected that the lettering was dirty and almost illegible. A city which once has had the spirit to paint its name for air travelers should maintain it properly.

Flying low to make out street signs is dangerous, yet often this has to be done. I dare say that in time legislation will take care of this problem. Possibly a uniform method will be adopted of placing names near a railroad or close to a main highway for easy recognition. Once names are looked for in a definite location, they are more easily picked up from the air.

"My compass reads due west. I have (Continued on page 195)

28

Thinks *When SHE'S* Flying

Later I bought a similar plane equipped with an experimental motor, the first one turned out by a western manufacturer. There were many "bugs" in it, as in all first products. Every flight was something of a test—and often a good deal of a surprise.

Adjustments and mechanical changes were forever being made.

Sometimes the engine overheated, sometimes it would spatter the pilot with oil or sometimes its vibration would tickle my feet so that I hardly could keep them on the rudder. Little by little these hilarious eccentricities were eradicated—a story typical of any mechanical development. It is just this sort of experimentation and day-by-day improvement through testing, that has produced the high quality of the motors and the planes of today.

Tabloided my autobiography is simple. As my father's law work was connected with railroads, the family moved about the country considerably; I think I graced seven high schools within the usual four years. With the war, I went to Toronto and worked as V. A. D. in a unit which corresponded to our nurses' aids.

That experience almost inspired me to be a physician and I followed it with pre-medical work at Columbia until conviction was borne home that I lacked the real "call" essential to medical success. Then California and my first flying. And East again to Boston in a few years for teaching and settlement work.

Flying for me has been both a sport and a commercial avocation. For a couple of years my connection with it has included a directorship in a commercial air-port where I have had some experience with the technical problems of the industry. Resulting from my modest activities in aviation came my election as vice-president of the Boston chapter of the National Aeronautic Association, just before the Friendship flight this summer.

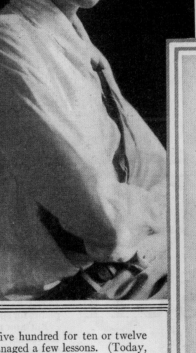

years since the war has seen great advancement. It was in 1920 that I began to learn to fly. My first flight, I remember, was at Rogers Airport, Los Angeles. I was there with my father and talked him into treating me to a ride. I found I wouldn't be trusted in the front cockpit alone. The pilot had impressed another to go along. Obviously I was considered a nervous lady who might become hysterical, try to jump or indulge some idiosyncrasy that men impute to women.

To me that was the beginning of active interest. As I sailed over the oil derricks indigenous to that part of California I knew I wanted to fly over them by myself. And I set about trying to. Prices for instruction had decreased from one thousand dollars to five hundred for ten or twelve hours in the air and after some high finance, I managed a few lessons. (Today, by the way, prices have been reduced by half again.)

New students were instructed in planes with dual controls, as they are now, the rudder and stick in the front cockpit being connected with those in the rear. Any false move the student makes can be corrected by the instructor. Every move is duplicated, always the experienced pilot commanding the situation.

In those days it was necessary for a woman to wear breeks and leather coats. The fields were dusty and the planes hard to enter. My leather coat of that period, by the way, I wore across the Atlantic this summer. After two and a half hours of instruction in the air I felt that I must have a plane of my own. It cost me two thousand dollars. To earn part of it I got my first job—with the telephone company. It was not an elaborate one, being a sort of chaperon to the office boys, and file clerk.

The end of that hard-earned plane was sad. I finally sold it to a young pilot who had been in the war but had not flown for some time. The day of the purchase he asked a friend to go up with him. Very close to the ground he began vertical banking to the horror of all who watched. The plane slipped and crashed and both men were killed—needlessly.

34

Amelia Earhart

When the National Association of Playgrounds instituted a model airplane tournament for youngsters, it asked me to be on the active committee in Boston and help judge at the finals in September. This activity, a meeting ground of social work and aviation, particularly appealed to me, but alas, flying the Atlantic curtailed my usefulness.

Similar incidents in my life have drawn me more and more towards aviation. The more I get into it, the more interest it holds. For me it combines the fun of any other sport with the fascination that comes from watching anything develop and form, whether it be a business, a personality or a sunset. Surely no one familiar with the romance of aviation's growth can fail to comprehend my enthusiasm for it.

"Try flying yourself."

That should be aviation's first commandment. The experience may mean little. Some people won't like it, and some will become enthusiasts. However, those who try it cannot fail to gain in understanding, which is always valuable.

"Try flying yourself." I believe that aviation could be sold more effectively under that slogan than under any other. Patronage would put an end to much guesswork and uncertainty and would establish flying as a business more firmly. Of course I am not overlooking the value of patronage of the express and mail sections.

To the men who have pioneered and produced the excellent motors and planes of today, we owe much. The people of America would indeed be ungrateful if they did not show their appreciation of the work of these pioneers by using what they produce.

How can we expect them to continue to do great things without encouragement?

Do you know that last year more

than two thousand commercial aeroplanes were constructed and operations in the commercial field approximated thirteen million miles of flying? Five thousand passengers were carried, and two and a half million pounds of freight transported, not to mention the notable attainments of the air-mail and the untabulated activity of private planes.

The interest of men in aviation has always been keen. No one has had more evidence of that fact than I. I have found too that they do not bottle up their enthusiasm—they share it with their families. A number of men have urged me to help them interest their wives or women friends in aviation and it is with these men in mind that I write now of women in aviation—a phrase that might well be changed more specifically to women outside of aviation.

The full effectiveness of woman's interest doesn't at all imply that all of them should become aviators. The more people who fly, women included, the better—but just *using* planes, not being at the controls, also counts almost as heavily. For every pilot there must be a half-dozen, a dozen or a score of passengers—men and women. The family car of today will be the family plane of tomorrow. It is natural to expect that, such being the case, a man will consider the taste and comfort of his wife or his sister as aviation becomes part of his life.

Today there are planes for carrying passengers, mail, express and freight. They are the modern note in traffic, comparable to electrical refrigerators, vacuum devices and other leisure-making appliances of the household.

In many fields women share the purchasing power. It is a brave man who buys one make of car when his wife wants another! Surely women's influence is primarily responsible for the rapid development of the American automobile in beauty and in comfort. The president of a well-known company told me the other day that the new models, at least as regarded outer attractiveness, were designed to appeal to the feminine eye. "American women keep us on our (*Continued on page 158*)

STEICHEN

Miss Amelia Earhart

A new portrait by Steichen
of the famed American flier
who is now the wife of Mr.
George Putnam, the publisher

13. Edward Steichen, Amelia Earhart, 1931 (for *Vanity Fair*, November 1931)

14. Edward Steichen, "Miss Amelia Earhart," 1931 (for *Vanity Fair*, November 1931)

15. Unidentified Photographer, Amelia Earhart, 1933

16. Edward Steichen, "Amelia Earhart Putnam—A Lady Lindbergh," *Vanity Fair*, July 1932

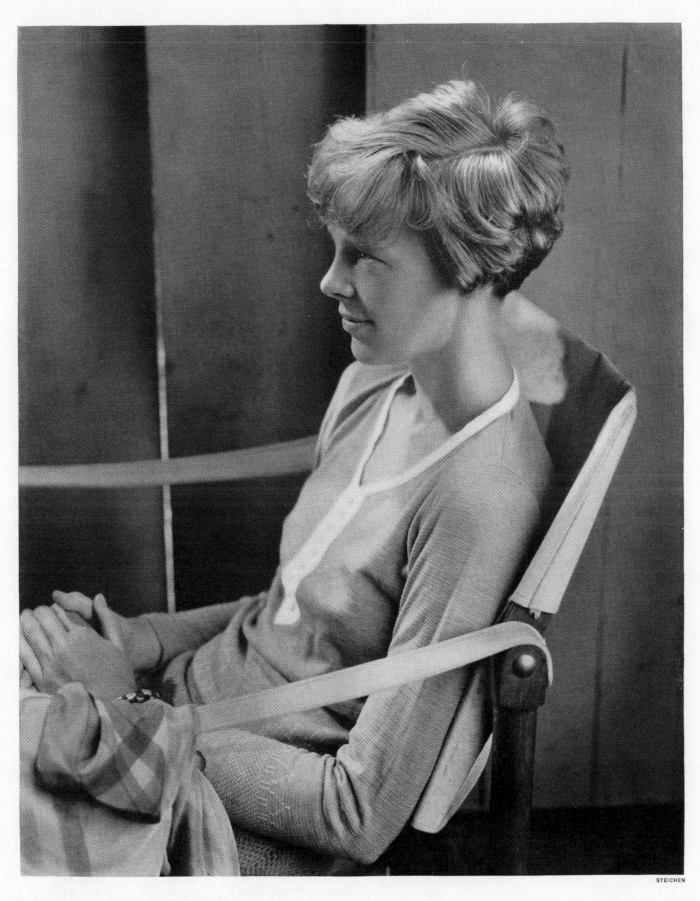

STEICHEN

A recent portrait of the world's premiere aviatrix, the first woman pilot to fly across the Atlantic alone

Amelia Earhart Putnam—A Lady Lindbergh

17. Unidentified Photographer, Amelia Earhart, June 22, 1931

18. Unidentified Photographer, Amelia Earhart, December 15, 1930

19. Unidentified Photographer, Amelia Earhart and George Palmer Putnam, September 16, 1935

20. Unidentified Photographer, Amelia Earhart and George Palmer Putnam at home in Rye, New York, ca. 1935

AMELIA EARHART

World's Premiere Aviatrix
The First Woman Pilot to Fly Across
the Atlantic Alone

On May 20, 1932, the fifth anniversary of Lindbergh's pioneer adventure, Amelia Earhart flew the Atlantic from Newfoundland to Ireland. Thus she became the first woman to have flown the Atlantic solo, just as she was the first woman to fly the Atlantic as a passenger. She set a speed record between the two continents and a new distance record for women. Also she became the second person ever to have crossed the Atlantic by air alone—the other being Lindbergh.

Since 1920 Amelia Earhart—who in private life is Mrs. George Palmer Putnam, wife of the New York publisher, explorer, author—has been a flyer. In 1928 she crossed on the famous "Friendship" flight. Thereafter, she has established many records for women. She was the first woman to make a transcontinental air crossing, and subsequently was the first person to take an autogiro across the continent, just as she was the first woman to solo an autogiro, holding also the autogiro altitude record. Later she established a new time record for a woman crossing the American continent by air.

Holds Important Aviation Positions

Miss Earhart is Vice-President of the National Aeronautical Association and has been prominently identified with many aviation activities. She was Vice-President and coöperated in the founding of an air-line between New York and Washington. She is a member of the National Contest Committee and of many other committees having to do with aviation and education.

Previous to the 1928 flight, Miss Earhart was associated with settlement work. Since then she has been aviation Editor of a national magazine and has written many articles. She is also the author of two books. The first, "Twenty Hours and Forty Minutes," is descriptive of the "Friendship" flight. Her second book is called "The Fun of it." In it she tells much of the story of her own life and her flying activities, of women and of aviation yesterday and today, and the story of her solo Atlantic flight.

Receives Distinguished Flying Cross

Following her flight to Ireland, Miss Earhart was accorded enthusiastic receptions at home and abroad. She has received honors from England, France, Italy and Belgium. In Rome she was received by Mussolini. In Brussels by the King and Queen of Belgium. In the United States she was accorded the Gold Medal of the National Geographic Society, and the President, by special resolution of Congress, bestowed upon her the Distinguished Flying Cross—the first woman to be so honored.

A Delightful Speaker

Miss Earhart is an accomplished speaker. Her charming use of words is as notable as the grace and modesty which have won for her the affectionate admiration of the world. In her lectures, she describes not only the Atlantic flight, but also tells of her other experiences, and of the meaning and possibilities of flying in general, especially as they relate to women. The story she tells holds a wealth of dramatic interest, always toned with whimsical humor.

Snapped Just Before Taking Off Alone
to Fly the Atlantic

LECTURE SUBJECT:
"Flying for Fun"

A SERIES --- JANUARY 30
B SERIES --- JANUARY 31

TUCSON HIGH SCHOOL AUDITORIUM

Tickets at College of Fine Arts

PRICE: $1.00 — $1.50 — $2.00

21. Flyer promoting Amelia Earhart's speaking engagement in Tucson, Arizona, ca. 1933

22. Ben Pinchot, Amelia Earhart, 1932

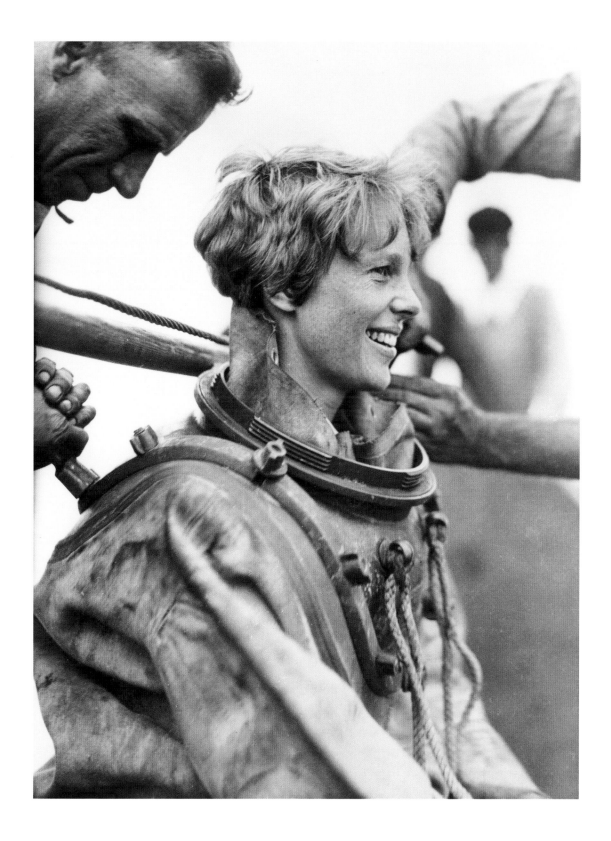

23. Unidentified Photographer, Amelia Earhart's first parachute drop, June 1935

24. Unidentified Photographer, Amelia Earhart goes deep sea diving, July 25, 1929

25. Unidentified Photographer, Amelia Earhart and Cary Grant, 1935

26. Unidentified Photographer, Amelia Earhart and Harpo Marx, July 1932

27. Unidentified Photographer, Amelia Earhart, ca. 1932

Women *and* Courage

Drawing by Clayton Knight

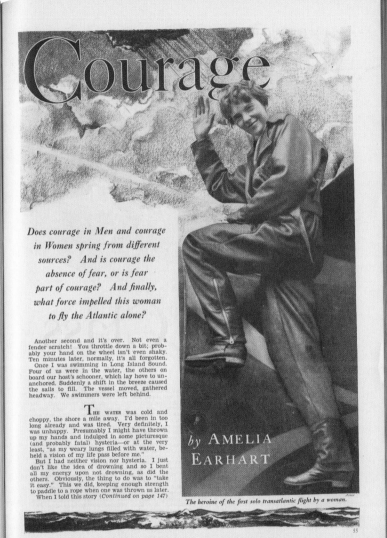

Does courage in Men and courage in Women spring from different sources? And is courage the absence of fear, or is fear part of courage? And finally, what force impelled this woman to fly the Atlantic alone?

by AMELIA EARHART

The heroine of the first solo transatlantic flight by a woman.

"HOW MUCH courage does it take for a woman to make a solo transatlantic flight?"

Since I brought my plane down in William Gallegher's field near Londonderry, after about fourteen hours of flying from Harbor Grace, Newfoundland, I have been asked that question scores of times. When I have evaded answering it—because, honestly, I can't tell the exact amount of courage required for that or for any other special feat—the questioners have probed deeper:

"When you took off, weren't you afraid? And later, when you saw flames shooting out about the exhaust, weren't you terrified?"

Well, in fiction one reads that in those final seconds when death seems sure the character's "entire life passes in review." That may be true in fiction. In real life, I do not know. I only know that no one who actually has come through a tight place and told me about it has confessed to such kaleidoscopic mental review.

I remember talking one day with a famous mail pilot. He had recently been in an accident. In a storm somewhere east of Cleveland one of the wings of his plane had come off. It all came about so swiftly, and in the dark and the rain, that at first he could not tell what had happened. Only that the plane was out of control.

"It must have been frightening," I said.

"Rot! Too busy for that at the time. I just wanted to be sure the ship was hopeless before I bailed out."

"What did you think about?" I asked.

The pilot scratched his head. "Gosh! I don't know. Mostly, I was thankful to have a parachute. The big thing was to get it and myself clear . . . While I was floating down through the dark—it's funny how quiet it was with the engine gone—there was plenty of time to think. I did worry a bit about where I'd land. I hoped it would be near a house. *I hate walking.*"

I tell this story because it epitomizes the type of thought that one is apt to have in moments of danger.

Perhaps it is then that apparent inconsequentials loom largest.

The sudden breath of imminent disaster galvanizes most people into a supreme effort to survive. Whether you are coward or hero, you do your best. And I doubt whether, under the tension of crisis, you think much about it. Usually in a pinch—whether it comes in the air, on land or in the water—there is so much that must be done, and *quickly*, that all effort goes into doing it; so there is no energy left, nor time, nor inclination, to feel your spiritual pulse in order to ascertain whether it beats to the tune of courage or of cowardice.

Think back, yourself. If you drive a car, I'm sure you've had some narrow squeaks. You're bowling along a fine highway, for instance, with no traffic (and no policemen!) in sight. Perhaps you've opened her up a bit—when suddenly, without warning, a truck roars out from a hidden side road. You both swerve; brakes grind; for a split second a smash looms, ugly, complete. You can see it all, and the consequences. Too bad!

But that isn't what you think about. You're too busy for thinking—too busy handling the wheel, the foot and emergency brakes, the throttle; too intent upon judging the exact last six inches between you and the ditch; too vividly focused upon the problems of appraising automatically your speed and the other fellow's, and judging how to slither by, cheating the seemingly inevitable.

Another second and it's over. Not even a fender scratch! You throttle down a bit; probably your hand on the wheel isn't even shaky. Ten minutes later, normally, it's all forgotten.

Once I was swimming in Long Island Sound. Four of us were in the water, the others on board our host's schooner, which lay hove to unanchored. Suddenly a shift in the breeze caused the sails to fill. The vessel moved, gathered headway. We swimmers were left behind.

THE WATER was cold and choppy, the shore a mile away. I'd been in too long already and was tired. Very definitely, I was unhappy. Presumably I might have thrown up my hands and indulged in some picturesque (and probably fatal) hysteria—or at the very least, "as my weary lungs filled with water, beheld a vision of my life pass before me."

But I had neither vision nor hysteria. I just don't like the idea of drowning and so I bent all my energy upon not drowning, as did the others. Obviously, the thing to do was to "take it easy." This we did, keeping enough strength to paddle to a rope when one was thrown us later.

When I told this story *(Continued on page 147)*

(Continued on page 147)

54   55

28. Amelia Earhart, "Women and Courage," *Cosmopolitan*, September 1932

29. Unidentified Photographer, Amelia Earhart, May 22, 1932

30. Unidentified Photographer, Amelia Earhart, May 22, 1932

31. Unidentified Photographer, Amelia Earhart, May 22, 1932

© Keystone View Company

RESIDENTS OF LONDONDERRY CHEER THE SUCCESSFUL TRANSATLANTIC FLYER AS SHE LANDS NEAR THEIR CITY AFTER HER LONG
AND DANGEROUS SOLO FLIGHT

© Harris and Ewing

A TRIBUTE FROM MRS. HOOVER

The "First Lady of the Air" was presented with an exquisite basket of
flowers by the First Lady of the Land.

Photograph from Keystone View Company

READY FOR A FLIGHT

That rare quality of courage, together with skill and a sureness of spirit,
is reflected in Miss Earhart's flying smile.

32. "The Society's Special Medal Awarded to Amelia Earhart," *National Geographic*, September 1932

33. Unidentified Photographer, Amelia Earhart and George Palmer Putnam, late May or early June 1932

34. "'Lady Lindy' Comes Home: Views of America's Reception for the First Woman to Fly the Atlantic Alone," *Mid-Week Pictorial*, July 2, 1932

THE PRESIDENT OF THE UNITED STATES HONORS
A DARING AVIATRIX: MR. HOOVER
Presenting the National Geographic Society Medal to
Mrs. Amelia Earhart Putnam at the White House in the
Presence of Mrs. Hoover and Gilbert Grosvenor (Left),
President of the Society.
(Times Wide World Photos, Washington Bureau.)

A FEW WORDS TO A NATION-WIDE AUDIENCE:
MRS. PUTNAM
Broadcasting a Message After Receiving the Cross of
Honor of the United States Flag Association at the
Federal Hall Reproduction in Bryant Park, New York.

THE CITY'S
MEDAL FOR
A DISTIN-
GUISHED
GUEST:
MAYOR
WALKER
Calling Attention
to the Decoration
Conferred on
Mrs. Putnam in
the City Hall
Ceremonies.

At Left—
WITH ALL THE
ACCOMPANI-
MENTS OF
MODERN
ACCLAIM:
THE PROCES-
SION
Nearing City
Hall, With
Camera Men and
Sound Techni-
cians Preceding
the Aviatrix's
Car to Record
the Proceedings.

NEW YORK ACCORDS A "LINDBERGH WELCOM
ACROSS THE ATLANTIC:
Riding Up the Broadway Canyon Through Cheering
Enroute to Her Official F

: VIEWS OF AMERICA'S
FIRST WOMAN TO
TIC ALONE

NEW YORK'S DISTINGUISHED GUEST APPEARS WITH AN ARMFUL OF ROSES: MRS. PUTNAM on the Steps of the City Hall With Mayor James J. Walker and a Group of the Leading Participants in the Official Reception.

E WOMAN WHO ACCOMPLISHED A SOLO FLIGHT ELIA EARHART PUTNAM
With the Traditional Accompaniment of Ticker Tape, the New York City Hall. (Times Wide World Photos.)

A SMILE FOR THE CHEERING CROWDS: MRS. PUTNAM Starting Up Broadway Accompanied by Charles L. Lawrance, President of the Aeronautical Chamber of Commerce.

At Right— GREETED BY COMRADES OF THE AIR: WOMEN FLIERS Welcoming the Transatlantic Aviatrix on Her Arrival From Europe Aboard the Ile de France. Left to Right Are Mae Holmes, Mrs. Ford G. Samson, Elvy Kalep, Mrs. Ruth Elder Camp, Mrs. John T. Remey, Mrs. Putnam, Elinor Smith and Viola Gentry.

IN THE FIRST STAGES OF THE CEREMONIES: THE AVIATRIX
With Her Husband, George Palmer Putnam, Posing for Photographs Aboard the Ile de France.

35. Advertisement for Lucky Strike cigarettes, 1928

Amelia M. Earhart, first woman to fly the Atlantic by aeroplane

says—

"Lucky Strikes were the cigarettes carried on the 'Friendship' when she crossed the Atlantic. They were smoked continuously from Trepassey to Wales. I think nothing else helped so much to lessen the strain for all of us."

"It's toasted"
No Throat Irritation-No Cough.

36. Unidentified Photographer, Macy's window display on "Safety and the Modern Air Liner," showcasing Amelia Earhart's luggage line, ca. 1933

37. "Designed by Amelia Earhart," *Woman's Home Companion*, August 1934 (photograph by Frederick Bradley)

Miss Earhart is not only a flyer. She is a designer too. The proof is here in a sports pattern, especially nice for school

PHOTOGRAPH BY FREDERICK BRADLEY

Amelia Earhart Pattern No. 5562. Two-piece Dress. Sizes, 14 to 20. Size 16 requires 1½ yards of 53-inch material for the blouse and 2 yards of 53-inch contrasting material for the skirt. Price of this pattern, 25 cents. Send your order (with stamps) to Woman's Home Companion, Service Bureau—P. 8, 250 Park Avenue, New York.

Designed by Amelia Earhart

IT WAS our intention not to mention the word "airplane" in connection with this youthful sports pattern designed by Amelia Earhart. Long before she ever stepped into a plane—when she was in high school in fact—Miss Earhart began making her own clothes. And she has kept right on making them ever since. To those who know her, therefore, it is no more surprising to see her launched as a successful designer than to see her winging her way over the ocean to Ireland.

But try as we may we can't leave the Lockheed Vega out of this. It is there in the background always, a sleek unfettered object, ready for action, symbol of the kind of clothes Amelia Earhart likes to wear and to design.

Miss Earhart, you see, doesn't think of us as reclining Madame Récamiers. We may not pilot a plane, we may not play opposite Tilden on the courts, but we do lead active lives, nearly all of us. And so she has set herself the task of designing clothes to fit—simple comfortable clothes, free of all extraneous hangings even in the evening.

This good-looking two-piece dress which you see pictured at the left is typical. You can take any inch of it from the simple gored skirt that is neither too full nor too narrow (everything Miss Earhart does must be right to the sixteenth of an inch) to the trim jacket-like top that fits in just so at the waist, and you won't find a detail that she doesn't swear by stoutly. The roll collar is one of her favorites and you can wear it with the button fastening pictured or with one of her neat ties, included in the pattern. The French cuff, the roomy shoulders—all of these are Earhart specials.

But the thing she likes most about this pattern (and you will too) is the two-piece theme. You can wear the skirt with other tops and the top with other skirts, Teens and Twenties please note. You can also work out a number of fabric and color combinations, just as interesting as this of checked and plain materials.

Miss Earhart chose a beige and brown check for the pull-over top and plain beige for the skirt—in one of the new fall heathery woolens, worked out in harmonizing plain and checked combinations—because she likes the quiet simplicity of beige and brown and because nothing is smarter for sports now than the checked top and plain skirt. You can choose other colors, however, in this same checked and plain combination—red and deep blue, yellow and brown. Or you can make the dress all in one soft feathery rust-colored woolen. Or again you may have a dark brown skirt and a bright green blouse. The buttons and belt would match the dark color and so would the hat and the shoes.

Miss Earhart's final suggestion has to do with the topcoat. Plan that to go with either the skirt or the blouse and you turn your two-piece dress into a practical three-piece suit.

● Amelia Earhart . . . Spanner of Oceans and Continents . . . Maker and Breaker of Records . . . Greatest Common Denominator of Mechanistic and Feministic Civilizations . . . Social Worker, Writer, Photographer . . . *At home, Mrs. George Palmer Putnam.*

PART OF THE FUN OF IT

by AMELIA EARHART

whose latest book is "The Fun of It"

I probably inherited from my father a talent for being an eyewitness. Things always happened when he was on the spot—not just after he left, or just before he arrived, as is Fate's annoying arrangement for so many people. If a building was going to burn, it burned when he was in it, or close by. If a woman was going to faint, she fainted in *his* arms.

Rather early in life I, too, noticed a predisposition for things to happen when I was around, though not in the grand manner of my sire. For the benefit of my friends who were too early or too late to be eyewitnesses, I faithfully lugged a camera everywhere I went for a good many years.

● Flying the Atlantic may have been brought a step nearer because of this habit—particularly after I began to realize the commercial advantage of picture making. In 1920 when I first took to flying, time in the air came high. One of the first extra rides earned by a camera, I remember, resulted from casually driving by a California oil field. Just as I passed, one of the wells "came in," blew men and fittings hither and yon and gushed blackly over the surrounding territory.

I stopped, of course, and was grinding away when interrupted by a neighboring real estate agent. Would I sell a copy of my movie film to show prospects what might happen on any of the lots they might purchase? I would—and had the fun of sailing over the very spot later, on the money paid for being on hand a few days before.

● Later, a little money for flying came from a regular but obscure job in a photographic studio. I helped develop and print pictures and now and then tried my hand at taking them.

I have always liked people's faces and those eventful few months made me see values in faces never recognized before. In fact, I think I must have become somewhat "arty" during this period for I saw character in everything. Even a garbage can had "it" if the shadows were right.

Having only two hands and two feet, I took no pictures on the Atlantic solo flight. Though most of the flying was at night, I saw enough in the daylight hours to wish for a camera. I do not mean scenery in the usual sense, but cloud formations. Beautiful and strange were these and unlike any I had seen on land. If I could have brought a pictorial record back with me, I might have added a little to the meteorological data slowly accumulating for the benefit of future passenger operations over the ocean.

One of the most exciting pictures I have ever made really does not look exciting at all. It is just an airplane picture of a boat. Lying flat on my tummy, I snapped it as the monoplane Friendship circled the S.S. America five years ago on the flight between Harbour Grace and Wales.

● For more than eighteen hours we three in the crew had been flying over the ocean. Since eight o'clock the previous evening, our radio had been silent.

According to our estimates, we *should* have been in sight of Ireland, but where Ireland ought to have been was fog, and occasional glimpses of water. Suddenly through an opening in the fog we saw a big transatlantic passenger vessel. However, instead of traveling parallel with our course, she was cutting across. If we were where we thought we were, west of Ireland, no transatlantic steamer should be behaving so. Were we lost? Should we play safe and land beside the ship, or continue?

With only a couple of hours' gasoline left, the answer to such questions might have spelled life or death to us. It was after we had decided to stake all on our somehow being right, that I took my exciting picture.

The explanation for the America's action was easy—afterward. We had passed Ireland and were over the Irish Sea, not the Atlantic. When we saw land, not long afterward, it was Wales. Though we didn't know that until we were told.

● Having lived a peripatetic life—never longer than four years in one place, with frequent lengthy excursions away from that, I suppose pictures mean more to me than to some people. They are stabilizers on a shifting world and tend to keep records straight and memories fresh.

The pleasure I might have felt as a child in having my picture taken has been somewhat dulled latterly through facing too many lenses. However, standing behind my own Ciné-Kodak directed at others is still a very real part of "the fun of it"!

A.E.

Note: With Ciné-Kodak, simplest of home movie cameras, you can take splendid movies of your own as easily as you now take snapshots. Any Ciné-Kodak dealer will gladly show sample reels of the kind that you yourself can make. The famous Model "K," Eastman's finest movie camera, "does everything." Takes telephoto movies. Wide-angle. Kodacolor (movies in full natural color). Indoor movies by daylight. Loads with full 100 feet of 16 mm. film. Eastman Kodak Company, Rochester, New York.

Below: "With frequent ,lengthy excursions away" . . . and if the flyer is a woman, she may see in Manhattan's dwindling towers a stunning fabric design.

Above: "I faithfully lugged a camera everywhere I went . . . I saw character in everything."

Left: "Lying flat on my tummy, I snapped it as the monoplane *Friendship* circled the *S.S. America* five years ago."

Right: "Standing behind my own Ciné-Kodak directed at others is still a very real part of 'the fun of it.'"

CINÉ-KODAK "K"

EASTMAN'S FINEST MOVIE CAMERA

"Having lived a peripatetic life". . . The "AE" everybody knows, starting on her first transcontinental solo flight.

38. Advertisement for Eastman's Ciné-Kodak camera, 1933 (photographs of Amelia Earhart by Victor Keppler)

39. Anton Bruehl, Amelia Earhart in a suit of her own design, 1934 (for *Vogue*, June 1934)

40. Frederick Bradley, Amelia Earhart with tailor and model, 1934

41. Frederick Bradley, Amelia Earhart in flying clothes of her own design, January 22, 1934

42. Unidentified Photographer, Amelia Earhart, January 4, 1935

43. Unidentified Photographer, Amelia Earhart, 1932–36

44. Unidentified Photographer, Amelia Earhart, 1931

45. Unidentified Photographer, Amelia Earhart and George Palmer Putnam, May 29, 1931

46. Unidentified Photographer, Amelia Earhart in rubber lifeboat, 1935

47. Unidentified Photographer, Amelia Earhart, Waikiki, Hawaii, 1935

48. Unidentified Photographer, Amelia Earhart in Mexican dress, April 1935

49. Unidentified Photographer, Diego Rivera and Amelia Earhart, April 1935

50. Unidentified Photographer, Amelia Earhart, Mexico, April 1935

51. Unidentified Photographer, Amelia Earhart, 1936

ELINOR SMITH

RUTH NICHOLS

AMELIA EARHART PUTNAM   LOUISE THADEN

When ladies take the air

■ A famous pilot once remarked, "You fly with the seat of your pants." This would seem to be a masculine knack—it really means that nerve and tenacity are quite as important as skill and imagination in the air. But women bring other virtues to this art—a delicate hand, independent spirit and the innate feminine trick of being able to change their minds with the wind. Here are seven who have equalled, and often surpassed the feats of crack male flyers. Amelia Earhart Putnam was the first woman to fly across the Atlantic; Louise Thaden won the First Transcontinental Derby; Elinor Smith yielded altitude and endurance records to Ruth Nichols, who also holds astonishing world records for speed and endurance. Florence Lowe Barnes is the sky-pilot wife of a minister; Gladys O'Donnell is winner of the Second Transcontinental Derby and Dorothy Hester, age eighteen, is America's outstanding woman stunt-flyer

FLORENCE LOWE BARNES

52. "When Ladies Take the Air," *Vanity Fair*, May 1932

53. Unidentified Photographer, Amelia Earhart, 1932

54. Unidentified Photographer, Amelia Earhart and Melba Beard, August 31, 1935

55. Unidentified Photographer, Amelia Earhart surrounded by trophies, August 4, 1936

56. Unidentified Photographer, Mrs. Bernita S. Matthews, Mrs. Harvey W. Wiley, Amelia Earhart, Miss Anita Pollitzer, and Miss Ruth Taunton, members of the National Women's Party, White House, Washington, DC, September 22, 1932

57. Unidentified Photographer, Amelia Earhart and Eleanor Roosevelt, April 30, 1933

58. Unidentified Photographer, Amelia Earhart and students, February 26, 1933

59. Unidentified Photographer, Amelia Earhart on her plane, July 21, 1936

60. Unidentified Photographer, Amelia Earhart and Purdue University students Virginia Gardener, Rufinia Sexton, Barbara Sweeney, Betty Spilman, Barbara Cook, Louise Schickler, Mary Ed Johnston, Dorothy Hewitt, Gaby D. Roe, and Mary L. Hinchman, September 27, 1936

61. Announcement of exclusive coverage of Amelia Earhart's 1937 flight, *New York Herald Tribune*, March 14, 1937

Amelia Earhart's Own Day-to-Day Story . . .

Flight Around the Equator

Amelia Earhart is going to fly the world's equator—she who first flew the Atlantic almost ten years ago, later flew it again alone, still later flew the Pacific and soloed the length and breadth of the United States.

The world has been flown a number of times. But never by a woman. Never around its equator. And never in an East-to-West continuous flight. She plans to begin her flight next Monday.

She will fly the world's full circumference. And not as a barnstorming adventure but as a practical test—a limit test —of all that is modern in scientific and aerial invention pitted against the longest world flight ever contemplated— 27,000 miles of it.

Her story . . . in three hops over the Pacific, a swing across British New Guinea and Australia, a line across the Malay Peninsula, an arc through India and Arabia, a jump across Africa and another across the South Atlantic—her story, as it happens, as told by her, will appear only in the New York Herald Tribune.

It will begin the day the Electra—her "flying laboratory" —glides out of Oakland and over the Golden Gate on its way to the longest continuous flight ever attempted by man —or woman.

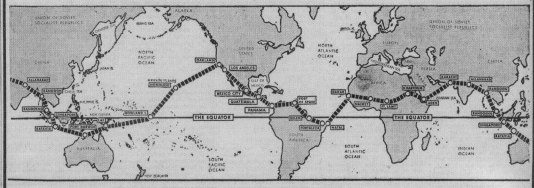

Exclusively in the

NEW YORK
Herald Tribune

A European edition is published daily in Paris

62. Unidentified Photographer, Paul Mantz, Amelia Earhart, Harry Manning, and Fred Noonan with photographers, 1937

63. Unidentified Photographer, Amelia Earhart showing the size of Howland Island, 1937

64. Unidentified Photographer, Amelia Earhart at the controls of her Lockheed Electra, March 12, 1937

65. Unidentified Photographer, Amelia Earhart and her Lockheed Electra above the Golden Gate Bridge, March 17, 1937

66. Unidentified Photographer, Amelia Earhart and George Palmer Putnam, May 29, 1937

67. Unidentified Photographer, Amelia Earhart and George Palmer Putnam, June 1, 1937

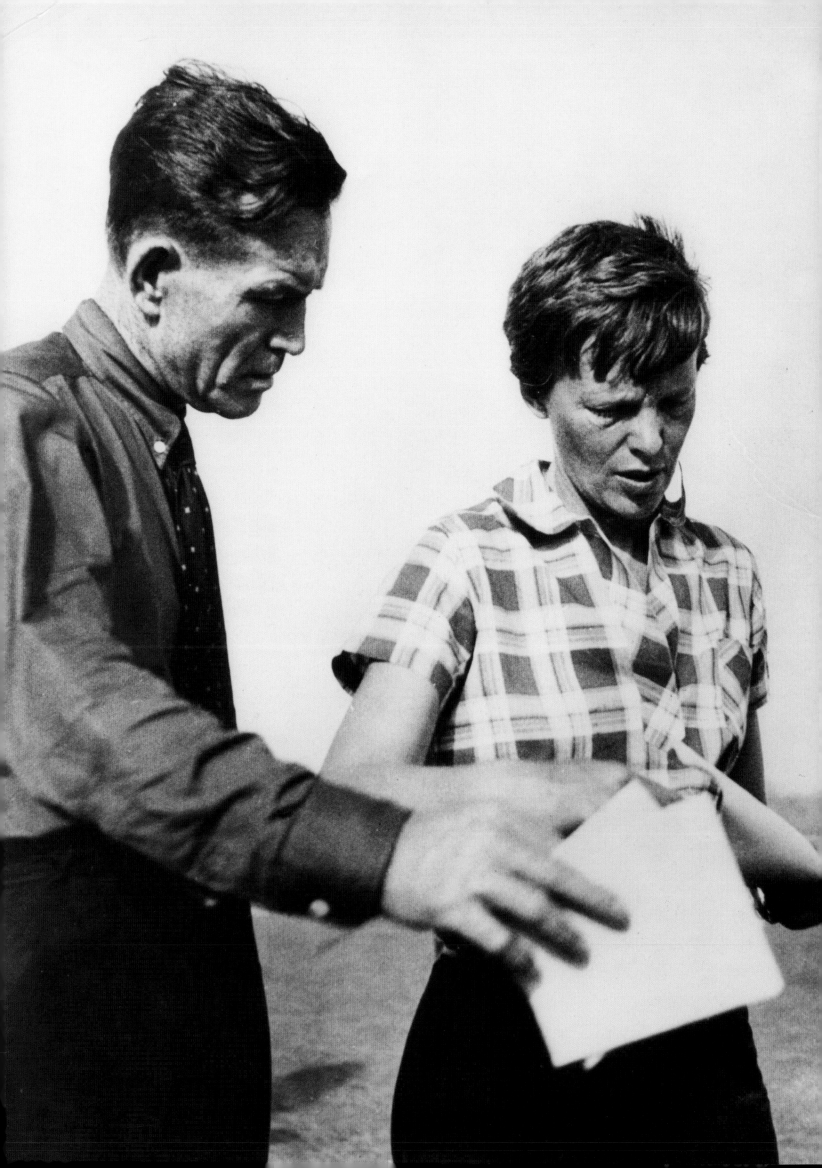

ASSOCIATED PRESS

68. Unidentified Photographer, Amelia Earhart and Fred Noonan, June 8, 1937

69. Unidentified Photographer, Amelia Earhart and Fred Noonan in Natal, Brazil, June 18, 1937

70. Unidentified Photographer, Amelia Earhart with camera, late June 1937

71. Unidentified Photographer, Amelia Earhart and Fred Noonan, late June 1937

"ANTICIPATION, I suppose, sometimes exceeds realization. Whatever the final outcome of the trip itself, certainly there was an extraordinary interest in the months of planning for it."

72. Page from Amelia Earhart's *Last Flight*, 1937

73. Albert L. Bresnik, Amelia Earhart in front of a map showing the route for her flight, 1937

74. Dick Whittington, Amelia Earhart, 1935, *Los Angeles Times*, July 18, 1937

75. Page of Amy Otis Earhart's scrapbook, 1937

76. Page of Amy Otis Earhart's scrapbook, 1939

She was not afraid!

AMELIA EARHART

("Dick" Whittington photo)

Missing Amelia Earhart
Declared Legally Dead

Los Angeles, Cal., Jan. 5.—(AP)—
Amelia Earhart, noted woman flyer
who disappeared on an around the
world flight in the summer of 1937,
was declared legally dead today. The
action was taken at the request of
the flyer's husband, George Palmer
Putnam, who received her personal
effects under terms of the will, dated
April 15, 1932. Miss Earhart provided for a trust fund, the income
from which goes to her mother, Mrs.
Amy Otis Earhart of Medford, Mass.

[1939]

LOG OF EARHART'S "LAST STUNT FLIGHT"

"When I've finished this job, I mean to give up long-distance stunt flying," confided Miss Earhart to friends before taking off on her round-the-world flight which ended somewhere in the Pacific. Because long-distance stunt flying does commercial aviation more harm than good, the Department of Commerce broke up the projected Lindbergh anniversary air race to Paris last May by refusing to permit the race to start in the U. S. When Miss Earhart disappeared and the U. S. Navy was put to heavy expense ($15,000 per day) searching for her with the battleship *Colorado* and the aircraft carrier *Lexington* (shown opposite), air commerce officials had a perfect case in point to justify their opposition to overwater flights which produce more personal publicity than sound aeronautical data. Herewith a log in pictures of the Earhart flight.

1 Official sponsor of the Earhart flight was Purdue University of Lafayette, Ind., which helped Miss Earhart raise the $80,000 to buy her Lockheed Electra (*above*). Miss Earhart was Purdue's consultant on Aeronautics and Careers for Women.

2 Miss Earhart's first plan was to fly the globe from west to east. In March, she flew from California to Honolulu. On her take-off for Howland Island, a tire blew out, the plane cracked up. Its landing gear was smashed, propellers were crumpled. No one was hurt.

3 Her "flying laboratory" reconditioned, Miss Earhart changed mind and direction, decided to head eastward around the world. With Frederick J. Noonan, former Pan American Airways navigator, she took off from Miami the gray morning of June 1.

4 After a stop in Puerto Rico, Miss Earhart jumped to Venezuela, lunched with local officials (*above*). Then she went on to Brazil, crossed to Africa. On her way over that continent, she telephoned this curious observation to her American newspapers: "In the central part of Africa that we've seen, highways appear entirely lacking."

5 In short, easy hops, the plane went to India, crossed to Batavia where this last picture of Pilot Earhart and Navigator Noonan was taken and radioed to America.

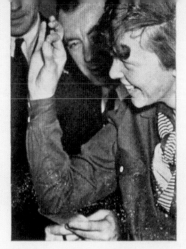

HOWLAND ISLAND
LATITUDE 0°49' NORTH
LONGITUDE 176°43' WEST
THIS ISLAND IS COLONIZED
THIS 30ᵀᴴ DAY OF MARCH
1935 BY AMERICAN CITIZENS
IN THE NAME OF THE UNITED
STATES OF AMERICA
NO TRESPASSING ALLOWED
HARRY L THEISS

6 Last Earhart stop before Honolulu was to be Howland Island. First claimed by the U. S. in 1860, it was reclaimed with the marker (*above*) when transpacific flying made Howland a potentially important air base.

7 "So big," said Miss Earhart when a reporter asked her, before her flight, how large Howland Island was.

8 Howland Island, two miles square, is a hard target to hit. No part of it rises more than 20 ft. above water. It has a small colony, a few shacks, a small runway.

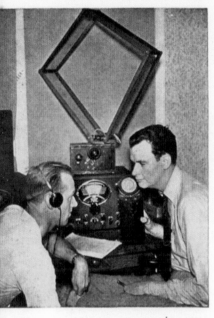

9 Radio messages thought to be from Earhart were picked up by amateur operators Pierson and MacNemany of Los Angeles.

10 Taken along were rubber boats, other safety devices. But the great failure of the Earhart equipment was the radio set which could not operate on a frequency to permit the cutter *Itasca*, waiting at Howland, to give Navigator Noonan his exact position.

11 "I would like to," said Assistant Commerce Secretary Johnson asked if he would forbid flight.

CONTINUED ON NEXT PAGE

YOUNGSTOWN OPENS CALUMET STEEL PLANTS TO 7000

The World Remembers • *Amelia's Exploits* • *As 'Last Hope' Hunt Starts*

HELEN MOODY AT TAHOE; MAPS NEV. DIVORCE

By United Press

RENO, July 13.—Helen Wills Moody, who for years was an international tennis champion, was settled in a rustic cottage on the shores of Lake Tahoe today to establish the six weeks residence required for a divorce in Nevada.

She already had conferred with Robert M. Price, prominent Reno divorce lawyer, and she admitted to reporters, after much cautious word bartering, that it was her intention to divorce Frederick S. Moody jr., oil executive and member of a prominent San Francisco family.

MOODY VACATIONS

They were married Dec. 23, 1929, after a romance that started on the French Riviera.

At the Moody home in San Francisco it was reported that he was on a two-weeks hunting vacation in northern California. It was his sister-in-law, Mrs. Corbitt Moody, of San Mateo, who first tipped off the news that the "Poker Face" of the tennis court expected to divorce her husband.

"Of course she went to Nevada to get a divorce," Mrs. Corbitt Moody said.

Armed with this statement, reporters forced the reluctant admission from the tennis star that she visited Attorney Price. That she had separated from her husband and that "once my mind is made up I see no reason for prolonging anything."

GROUNDS UNDECIDED

She was asked what grounds she would charge in a divorce suit, and answered that she supposed "anything like that would be up to Mr. Price."

Mrs. Moody arrived yesterday at fashionable Glenbrook with her Sealyham dog and enough baggage for a prolonged visit.

A possible rift between the Moodys long had been rumored, but was denied consistently by Mrs. Moody until her arrival here.

She laughed when asked if there was another romance in her life.

"People get so many funny ideas," she said.

TWO STABBED IN DOWNTOWN CHASE

After a wild chase during which two men suffered severe stab wounds, Joe Martinez, 14-year-old burglary suspect, today was finally captured by a group of irate citizens from whom officers were forced to rescue him.

Martinez, according to police reports, entered a clothing store at 328 South Main street, grabbed seven shirts of the counter and ran out into the street. Ralph Van Zant, 23, of 1320½ North Edgemont, clerk in the store, ran after him and using football tactics, tackled him, but was severely stabbed in the abdomen when Matinez drew a pocket knife with a seven-inch blade, police said.

Seeing the fallen clerk, a citizen, Harry F. Robinson, 35, 286 East Sixtieth street, took after the fleeing boy, but was severely stabbed in the hand when he attempted to grab him, the report read. Martinez then was caught by a group of angered citizens who knocked him down and kicked him just as police arrived upon the scene, it was reported.

As navy planes today launch the "last hope" hunt in the South Pacific for Amelia Earhart the world recalls her exploits. She is shown after she spanned the Atlantic in 1932, the first woman to do it alone.

After her triumphal return from Europe Miss Earhart won new laurels in aviation. She's shown after setting a new women's cross-country record from Los Angeles to New York in July, 1932.

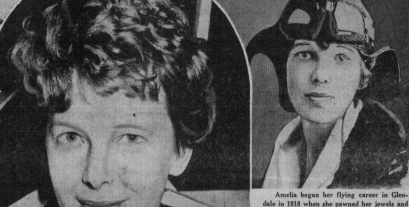

Amelia began her flying career in Glendale in 1918 when she pawned her jewels and furs to buy her first plane. She's shown in her first flying togs.

Because she looks so much like Charles Lindbergh and her record has paralleled his, she is often called "Lady Lindy." She is shown at left, Lindbergh at right.

Amelia is pictured with her husband, George Palmer Putnam, wealthy publisher, whom she wed in 1931. Now he is in Los Angeles closely following the flight of navy planes seeking her in South Pacific wastes.

LAST OF STRIKE BOUND MILLS TO OPEN

By Associated Press

EAST CHICAGO, Ind., July 13.—Youngstown Sheet and Tube C threw open the gates of its Calumet District steel plants today for all of its 7000 employes who desire to return to work.

The reopening, after a shutdown of 46 days, signalized resumption of operations by the last of the strike-bound plants in northern Indiana.

Leaders of the Steel Workers Organizing Committee, which called the strike and their followers hailed the reopening as a Committee for Industrial Organization victory, but their claims were disputed by the company and the Association of Steel Employes, an independent union.

Governor M. Clifford Townsend of Indiana declared the company and the S. W. O. C. had come to terms. Vice President J. C. Argetsinger of Sheet and Tube said the company had made no agreement and had granted concessions to no one.

The lack of understanding was reflected in the actions of strikers. On three occasions yesterday pickets massed about the firm's Indiana Harbor plant only to be called away by their leaders.

'SATISFACTORY POLICY'

Governor Townsend said the company voluntarily submitted a satisfactory labor policy to the S. W. O. C. and that it therefore was morally obligated to abide by that policy.

The company announced it would post signs at its plants stating the reopening was the result of demands by employes and not through any pressure by or agreement with the Steel Workers Organization Committee.

Van A. Bittner, Steel Workers Organization Committee regional director, announced the Committee for Industrial Organization had won a victory "through the truce arranged by Governor Townsend." His announcement was the signal for "victory" celebrations.

At the same time H. O. Brown, president of the Association of Steel Employes, declared it was victory for that organization.

Rivalry between the two labor organizations was blamed by police for a fight yesterday in front of the independent union's headquarters. One man was severely beaten. Three men were arrested.

(For other strike news see Page A-8.)

HOUSE OVERRIDES FARM LOAN VETO

By Associated Press

WASHINGTON, July 13.—The House override today President Roosevelt's veto of a bill to continue low interest rates on farm loans for two more years.

With a two-thirds majority those voting required to override, Speaker Bankhead announced the vote was 260 to 97.

The Senate has yet to act.

House action came after an hour's debate during which the chief executive's objections to the legislation were criticized and defended.

It was the second time this session the House had overridden a veto. Several weeks ago it joined the Senate in overriding legislation extending the time in which World War veterans might convert term life insurance policies.

After her first Pacific flight, Miss Earhart won new fame by being the first woman to fly from Los Angeles to Mexico City. She's shown in a tumultuous reception in Mexico City. On this flight she was blinded by an insect in her eye. Then she set a record in her solo flight from Mexico City to New York.

The Pacific ocean had claimed the lives of 10 intrepid fliers when Miss Earhart determined to be the first woman to make the Hawaii-Oakland flight. She is shown being greeted after completing the hop in 1935.

Out of her flying togs Miss Earhart always was as charmingly feminine as any woman dreams to be. She is shown above in a lacy evening gown. Between flights she rested in her home near Los Angeles.

Misfortunes have never bothered Miss Earhart. She's shown with Fred Noonan, navigator now lost with her, on the wing of her $75,000 "flying laboratory" after it crashed in Hawaii. She had it repaired and started her world flight anew. Known as the "smiling aviatrix," she sought to glorify aviation.

77. "Log of Earhart's 'Last Stunt Flight,'" *Life*, July 19, 1937

78. "World Remembers," *Los Angeles Herald and Express*, July 13, 1937

79. Unidentified Photographer, Twenty-foot snow statue of Amelia Earhart, Virginia, Minnesota, February 1938

80. Unidentified Photographer, Amelia Earhart on the wing of her plane, 1937/1945

81. Unidentified Photographer, Amelia Earhart at a Japanese tea ceremony, Hawaii, 1935/1970

WHEN HE "HAS
A HEADACHE"—
SURVIVING
SEXUAL
REJECTION

FOR KIDS:
NEW LIST OF
NONSEXIST
BOOKS

CUSTODY
PLANS
THAT WORK

"TRASHING"
READERS
TALK BACK

MATH ANXIETY:
NINE OUT OF TEN
WOMEN HAVE IT

CONFESSIONS OF
A NOT-SO-HAPPY
HOOKER

THE OTHER
BEAUTY CONTESTS:
TODDLERS IN
FALSE EYELASHES

SEPTEMBER/1976 $1.00

Ms.

BETTER THAN THE MYTH:
AMELIA EARHART
PLUS: T-SHIRT IRON-ON

14255

82. Unidentified Photographer, Irene Bolam, 1970

83. *Ms.*, September 1976

Amelia Earhart wore khakis.

GAP
KHAKIS

84. Advertisement for Gap khakis, 1993

85. Advertisement for Apple Inc., 1998

1. Jake Coolidge
Amelia Earhart, from the "Lady Lindy" series, June 1928
Gelatin silver print
Image and paper: 7 9/16 x 5 11/16 in. (19.2 x 14.5 cm)
The New York Times Photo Archives

Earhart's first Atlantic crossing in 1928 was sponsored by Amy Guest, an American heiress living in England who had wanted to make the flight herself. Her family balked and she agreed to back out as long as a suitable American female replacement could be found. Earhart, who had been flying since 1921, was selected by publisher George Palmer Putnam and publicist Hilton Railey.

Before Earhart's historic flight, Putnam arranged a deal with Paramount News for exclusive newsreel footage in both Boston and Trepassey, Newfoundland. Paramount photographer Jake Coolidge photographed Earhart on the roof of the Copley Plaza Hotel in Boston. In an attempt to link the young aviator with Charles Lindbergh, who, in the previous year, was the first person to successfully cross the Atlantic, Coolidge used this portrait session to draw attention to Earhart's physical and sartorial similarities to Lindbergh. Images from this "Lady Lindy" series were widely reproduced in the press for years; Earhart was never able to shake the nickname.

2. "Boston Girl Starts for Atlantic Hop," *New York Times*, June 4, 1928
Newspaper
22 1/2 x 17 3/4 in. (57.2 x 45.1 cm)
International Center of Photography, Museum Purchase

Earhart was not exactly the "Boston Girl" trumpeted by the headlines. Born and raised in Kansas, the thirty-year-old had been a nurse in Toronto, a pre-med student at Columbia University, and a settlement worker at Denison House in Boston before becoming the first woman to cross the Atlantic in an airplane.

On this front page of the *New York Times*, Amelia Earhart is presented in a pictorial convention that was followed throughout her career: a before-and-after spread with an image of Earhart in a school-girlish dress paired with a picture of the flyer in a leather jacket, trousers, and boots. The image on the left is from the "Lady Lindy" series by photographer Jake Coolidge (see cat. nos. 1 and 3).

3. Jake Coolidge
Amelia Earhart, from the "Lady Lindy" series, June 1928
Gelatin silver print
Image: 9 5/8 x 7 1/2 in. (24.5 x 19.1 cm); paper: 10 x 8 in. (25.4 x 20.3 cm)
The New York Times Photo Archives

"Our lady of the clouds: This newest 'Flying Flapper' (if so we may venture to call her) is Miss Amelia Earhart, a Boston society girl. On June 3 she flew from Boston to Halifax, N.S., as co-pilot with Wilmer Stultz and Lou Gordon, in a tri-motored Fokker monoplane, the ultimate objective of the flight being England."

4. Unidentified Photographer
Amelia Earhart, Wilmer Stultz, and Lou Gordon, early June 1928
Gelatin silver print
Image: 7 5/8 x 9 3/4 in. (19.4 x 24.8 cm); paper: 7 15/16 x 9 15/16 in. (20.2 x 25.2 cm)
The New York Times Photo Archives

As part of an extensive pre-flight publicity campaign, Putnam arranged a number of photo sessions in Boston before the *Friendship* crew left for Trepassey. In most of the advance photographs, Earhart is seen in flying clothes, even though she did not do any of the flying on the trip; officially she was the flight's co-pilot. Here, she strikes a surprisingly contemporary model-like pose, wearing her flight helmet, wool sweater, and leather jacket. The men, on the other hand, are dressed in elegant suits rather than flight clothes, heightening the contrast with Earhart's decidedly nonfeminine attire.

5. *New York Times,* June 10, 1928
Newspaper
22 7/16 x 16 3/8 in. (57 x 41.6 cm)
International Center of Photography, Museum Purchase

Putnam, who published Charles Lindbergh's *We* after the aviator's historic 1927 Atlantic crossing, arranged exclusive rights for Earhart's story to appear in the *New York Times.* Weeks before the flight, the *Times* began running images of Earhart alongside the *Friendship*'s pilot Wilmer Stultz and mechanic Lou Gordon in its weekly rotogravure picture section.

6. *New York Times,* July 1, 1928
Newspaper
22 7/16 x 16 3/8 in. (57 x 41.6 cm)
International Center of Photography, Museum Purchase

Near the end of the Atlantic flight, the *Friendship* began to run out of fuel, and Stultz landed the plane in Burry Port, Wales, rather than in Southampton as planned. Due to the lack of commotion caused by the landing, no one came to meet Earhart and the crew for over an hour. They were eagerly greeted in Southampton the following day by thousands of onlookers, including the female mayor of the city and Amy and Frederick Guest, who wanted to catch a glimpse of the first woman to cross the Atlantic.

The *New York Times* continues the convention of reproducing two contrasting images of Earhart, one in flying gear and one in "women's wear." "The changes London made in a famous aviator: Miss Amelia Earhart, who arrived in her flying suit and helmet, appeared for the first of the celebrations in her honor dressed in 'mufti.'" In this case, her civilian clothes were ill fitting because they were borrowed. Demonstrating her modesty, Earhart traveled in boots, breeches, a leather jacket, sweater, and a silk aviator's scarf; she did not bring a dress.

7. Unidentified Photographer
Amelia Earhart in her Ascot gown at the home of Amy Guest, late June 1928
Gelatin silver print
Image: 9 9/16 x 7 9/16 in. (24.3 x 19.2 cm); paper: 10 x 7 15/16 in. (25.4 x 20.2 cm)
The New York Times Photo Archives

Earhart did not pack many clothes for the crossing and relied on her hosts to provide suitable attire for various occasions. She is barely recognizable in this highly airbrushed photograph.

8. Page from Amelia Earhart's *20 Hrs. 40 Min.,* showing Earhart, Wilmer Stultz, and Lou Gordon, 1928
Book
8 1/4 x 5 3/4 x 1 3/8 in. (21 x 14.6 x 3.5 cm)
Collection of Ann L. Morse

In *20 Hrs. 40 Min.,* Earhart tells the story of the 1928 *Friendship* flight. As with Lindbergh's *We,* Earhart's book needed to be published as soon as possible after her return to the United

States so that she and Putnam could capitalize on her fame.

While most of the images of Earhart and her crewmates reproduced in the press were flattering, these outtakes testify to Earhart's sense of humor about her presentation as a media sensation. As the cult of celebrity grew, Earhart (and Putnam) were savvy about her image but careful not to make her seem too extraordinary to the public.

9. Unidentified Photographer
Amelia Earhart with a bouquet presented to her at the Boston airport, July 1928
Airbrushed gelatin silver print
Image: 10 x 7 1/2 in. (25.4 x 19.1 cm); paper: 10 x 8 in. (25.4 x 20.3 cm)
The New York Times Photo Archives

This image ran on the cover of the July 21, 1928, *Mid-Week Pictorial,* the rotogravure section of the *New York Times.* The headline read: "The first of her sex to fly the Atlantic Ocean: Miss Amelia Earhart, a Boston girl, comes back to Boston with a record that will always stand, for no other woman can be 'the first' to do what she did; and Boston greets her with open arms and a great popular demonstration. Here she is with the huge bouquet presented to her when she landed at the Boston airport from New York."

10. Unidentified Photographer
Amelia Earhart, 1930
Gelatin silver print
Image: 9 1/2 x 7 1/2 in. (24.1 x 19.1 cm); paper: 10 x 8 in. (25.4 x 20.3 cm)
Courtesy Condé Nast Archives

Several months after the *Friendship* flight, Earhart broke off her engagement to Sam Chapman. She and Putnam had begun to spend time together; the publisher/publicist accompanied Earhart to many receptions and she completed the manuscript for her first book, *20 Hrs. 40 Min.*, at the home of Putnam and his wife. She even dedicated the book to Dorothy Binney Putnam. The couple divorced in 1929 and Putnam pursued Earhart in earnest. Although Earhart was extremely wary of marriage, she and Putnam obtained a marriage license on November 8, 1930.

This portrait—not a typical engagement picture—was used by the *New York Times* to announce Earhart's marriage to Putnam. A small ceremony was held on February 7, 1931, at the home of Putnam's mother in Noank, Connecticut. Earhart and Putnam returned to work the following Monday. Although legally she took her husband's last name, the press used both her married and maiden names. Between Earhart and Putnam, however, she remained "A.E."

11. Amelia Earhart, "What Miss Earhart Thinks When She's Flying," *Cosmopolitan*, December 1928
Magazine spread: 11 5/8 x 17 in. (29.5 x 43.2 cm)
International Center of Photography, Museum Purchase

Cosmopolitan jumped at the chance to engage Earhart's celebrity. As the magazine's aviation editor, Earhart answered readers' questions about flying and the burgeoning commercial aviation industry. She also sought to normalize the experience of flying (her mother enjoyed a good book as she flew across the country, everyone will be commuting by autogiro in the future) and encouraged women to become "air-minded," promoting the idea that aviation represented the pinnacle of modernity and progress that could bridge distances and bring cultures together.

12. Amelia Earhart, "Try Flying Yourself," *Cosmopolitan*, November 1928
Magazine spread: 11 5/8 x 17 in. (29.5 x 43.2 cm)
International Center of Photography, Museum Purchase

Earhart published her first article as *Cosmopolitan*'s aviation editor in the November 1928 issue.

13. Edward Steichen
Amelia Earhart, 1931
For *Vanity Fair* (November 1931)
Gelatin silver contact print
Image: 9 7/8 x 7 15/16 in. (25.3 x 20.3 cm)
George Eastman House, Bequest of Edward Steichen by Direction of Joanna T. Steichen, 1979:2160:0004

14. Edward Steichen
"Miss Amelia Earhart," 1931
For *Vanity Fair* (November 1931)
12 3/4 x 9 7/8 x 3/16 in. (32.4 x 25.1 x 0.5 cm)
International Center of Photography, Museum Purchase

This image was published in the November 1931 *Vanity Fair* with the caption: "Miss Amelia Earhart. A new portrait by Steichen of the famed American flier who is now the wife of Mr. George Putnam, the publisher."

Although Earhart was a continuous source of fascination for human-interest journalists, she did not sit for many of the leading photographers of the day. Other than a few portraits by Edward Steichen, the foremost celebrity and fashion photographer on the Condé Nast staff, and mass-market image distributors like Underwood & Underwood, most pictures of Earhart were taken by little-known staff photographers at newspapers or wire services.

15. Unidentified Photographer
Amelia Earhart, 1933
Gelatin silver print
Image: 9 3/8 x 7 1/4 in. (23.8 x 18.4 cm); paper: 10 3/16 x 8 in. (25.9 x 20.3 cm)
The New York Times Photo Archives

This photograph was used for the cover of the January 7, 1933, *Mid-Week Pictorial*. "The outstanding aviation star of 1932. Amelia Earhart, whose lone flight across the Atlantic created a worldwide sensation and who added to her laurels by setting a new transcontinental record for women."

16. Edward Steichen
"Amelia Earhart Putnam—A Lady Lindbergh," *Vanity Fair*, July 1932
Magazine
12 5/8 x 9 3/4 x 1/8 in. (32.1 x 24.8 x 0.3 cm)
International Center of Photography, Museum Purchase

"A recent portrait of the world's premiere aviatrix, the first woman pilot to fly across the Atlantic alone."

This issue of *Vanity Fair* appeared in July 1932, shortly after Earhart returned from her record-breaking flight.

17. Unidentified Photographer
Amelia Earhart, June 22, 1931
Airbrushed gelatin silver print
Image: 9 3/4 x 7 13/16 in. (24.8 x 19.8 cm); paper: 10 x 8 in. (25.4 x 20.3 cm)
The New York Times Photo Archives

"The first woman to cross the continent in an autogiro. Amelia Earhart Putnam, the first woman to cross the Atlantic in a plane, lands her 'flying windmill' at the Oakland Airport after ten days of leisurely hops from Newark, N.J."

18. Unidentified Photographer
Amelia Earhart, December 15, 1930
Gelatin silver print
Image: 8 3/8 x 6 11/16 in. (21.3 x 17 cm); paper: 9 x 7 1/8 in. (22.9 x 18.1 cm)
International Center of Photography, The LIFE Magazine Collection

Earhart was rarely pictured with an open-mouthed grin. This image, however, seems to exemplify her attitude toward flying, as well as the title of her second book, *The Fun of It.* Throughout her career, Earhart maintained that she flew, not for fame or fortune, but because she loved it.

19. Unidentified Photographer
Amelia Earhart and George Palmer Putnam, September 16, 1935
Gelatin silver print
Image: 8 9/16 x 6 7/16 in. (21.7 x 16.4 cm); paper: 9 3/16 x 7 in. (23.3 x 17.8 cm)
International Center of Photography, The LIFE Magazine Collection

"Amelia Earhart, the aviator, deserts her plane for the moment, and serves her husband, George Palmer Putnam, breakfast in their new home in the Toluca Lake [Los Angeles] district. Palmer [sic] sagely commented that Miss Earhart has 'gone domestic—for a couple of minutes, anyway.'"

20. Unidentified Photographer
Amelia Earhart and George Palmer Putnam at home in Rye, New York, ca. 1935
Gelatin silver print
Image and paper: 10 x 8 in. (25.4 x 20.3 cm)
The Schlesinger Library, Radcliffe Institute, Harvard University

Earhart and Putnam worked together to promote the aviator's career. Many publicity shots, such as this one, show the pair either engaged in activities at home or at an airport. Photographers often complained that Putnam was always trying to weasel his way into their shots of Earhart.

21. Flyer promoting Amelia Earhart's speaking engagement in Tucson, Arizona, ca. 1933
Top photograph by Ben Pinchot
11 1/16 x 8 in. (28.1 x 20.3 cm)
International Center of Photography, Museum Purchase

Putnam organized an extensive and sometimes grueling tour of speaking engagements across the country. These lectures, which usually paid about $250, provided income as well as continued exposure for Earhart. During these talks, Earhart would publicize her latest book or flight and would also discuss topics such as women's issues and the importance of aviation.

The front of this flyer reproduces Ben Pinchot's studio portrait of the aviator in a velvet dress, pearls, and her honorary major's pin. The back pairs this image with one of Earhart clad in her flying suit, standing on her plane before the historic 1932 solo flight across the Atlantic.

22. Ben Pinchot
Amelia Earhart, 1932
Gelatin silver print
Image: 9 5/8 x 7 1/2 in. (24.4 x 19.1 cm); paper: 10 1/8 x 8 in. (25.7 x 20.3 cm)
International Center of Photography, The LIFE Magazine Collection

A variant image from Ben Pinchot's portrait session, this was one of the most widely circulated publicity photos of Earhart.

23. Unidentified Photographer
Amelia Earhart's first parachute drop, June 1935
Gelatin silver print
Image: 8 7/16 x 6 1/2 in. (21.4 x 16.5 cm); paper: 9 1/16 x 7 in. (23 x 17.8 cm)
The New York Times Photo Archives

"The woman who has made solo flights over two oceans experiments in New Jersey with a device for beginners and 'jumps' off a tower from a height of 115 feet."

Flying was an expensive endeavor and the only way to raise money and finance future flights was to keep Earhart in the public eye. Between record-breaking flights, whenever possible, Putnam orchestrated press opportunities for Earhart such as this parachute jump. Photographs from this event were reproduced on the cover of the June 8, 1935, *Mid-Week Pictorial* and this particular image was even distributed as a poster to schools.

24. Unidentified Photographer
Amelia Earhart goes deep sea diving, July 25, 1929
Gelatin silver print
Image and paper: 8 x 5 5/16 in. (20.3 x 13.5 cm)
National Archives and Records Administration

"An aviator learns the thrills of deep diving: Miss Amelia Earhart, still the only woman to fly the Atlantic, emerges from the bottom of the sea off Block Island."

Putnam was a tireless promoter of his newest celebrity and made sure that any of her unusual activities, like diving off the privately owned submarine *Defender*, were photographed and publicized. In addition to appearing in the *New York Times*, the photograph was published in Earhart's November 1929 column for *Cosmopolitan*, "Miss Earhart's Adventure on the Floor of the Sea." These events, combined with the stories of her flights, strengthened the idea that she was a courageous woman willing to tackle any adventure.

25. Unidentified Photographer
Amelia Earhart and Cary Grant, 1935
Gelatin silver print
Image: 9 1/4 x 7 1/4 in. (23.5 x 18.4); paper: 9 1/2 x 7 1/4 in. (24.1 x 18.4 cm)
Picture Collection, The Branch Libraries, The New York Public Library, Astor, Lenox and Tilden Foundations

In 1932, Putnam accepted a position as director of Paramount's editorial board and he and Earhart began living part of each year in Los Angeles. Between flights, Earhart spent time on the Paramount lot with Hollywood celebrities. She and Putnam recognized the need to keep her face in the papers; new connections with film stars only increased her glamour.

26. Unidentified Photographer
Amelia Earhart and Harpo Marx, July 1932
Gelatin silver print
Image: 8 7/16 x 6 1/2 in. (21.4 x 16.5 cm); paper: 8 15/16 x 7 in. (22.7 x 17.8 cm)
The New York Times Photo Archives

"Amelia Earhart Putnam, the woman flyer who conquered the Atlantic alone, had her first peek behind the scenes of the motion picture industry today with Harpo Marx, the blond member of the Marx foursome, those merry, mad comedians, as her guide. George Palmer Putnam, the publisher-husband of the great pilot, is to be a story executive in the studio, so 'Lady Lindy' wished to learn the methods used in production. Miss Earhart is shown above delightedly listening to the jesting of Harpo on the lot."

27. Unidentified Photographer
Amelia Earhart, ca. 1932
Gelatin silver print
Image: 7 9/16 x 5 5/8 in. (19.2 x 14.3 cm); paper: 8 1/8 x 6 in. (20.6 x 15.2 cm)
International Center of Photography, The LIFE Magazine Collection

28. Amelia Earhart, "Women and Courage," *Cosmopolitan*, September 1932

Magazine spread: 11 5/8 x 17 in. (29.5 x 43.2 cm)
International Center of Photography, Museum Purchase

The layout, which pairs a full-length portrait of Earhart in her flight suit with a gauzy headshot, parallels her text on courage. After declaring that fortitude is not based on sex, she suggests that she is "running the risk of becoming a heavy-handed feminist . . . I'm guilty, as I do become increasingly weary of male superiority unquestioned."

29. Unidentified Photographer
Amelia Earhart, May 22, 1932
Gelatin silver print
Image: 6 9/16 x 8 7/16 in. (16.7 x 21.4 cm); paper: 7 x 9 1/16 in. (17.8 x 23 cm)
The New York Times Photo Archives

"May of 1932 and the first woman to fly solo across the Atlantic. Miss Earhart atop her monoplane in a field outside Londonderry, Ireland, preparing to continue on to London after the flight which caused her to be acclaimed as 'Lady Lindy.'"

Flying from Harbor Grace in Newfoundland to Londonderry in thirteen and a half hours with a broken altimeter, Earhart set records for fastest Atlantic crossing and women's distance, exactly five years after Lindbergh's solo flight. The reception for her second Atlantic crossing was quite different than the first: no one was present for Earhart's historic landing in a pasture in Ireland on May 21, 1932. However, Earhart and her Lockheed Vega were mobbed by well-wishers and photographers the following morning, when this picture was taken. Earhart, unlike some other flyers, was particularly friendly with the press and was willing to reenact events specifically for their cameras.

30. Unidentified Photographer
Amelia Earhart, May 22, 1932
Gelatin silver print
Image: 7 5/8 x 11 1/8 in (19.4 x 28.3 cm); paper: 7 5/8 x 11 3/8 in. (19.4 x 28.9 cm)
The New York Times Photo Archives

"Braving the crowds at Hanworth: Mrs. Putnam with Ambassador [Andrew] Mellon at the club house entrance after her arrival from Londonderry."

After her solo flight across the Atlantic, Earhart flew to London and stayed with the ambassador and his family at the American Embassy.

31. Unidentified Photographer
Amelia Earhart, May 22, 1932
Gelatin silver print
Image and paper: 10 9/16 x 8 5/8 in. (26.8 x 21.9 cm)
The New York Times Photo Archives

This image appeared on the June 11, 1932, cover of the *Mid-Week Pictorial*. "London cheers the first woman to fly the Atlantic alone. Mrs. Amelia Earhart Putnam waving to the crowds which greeted her at Hanworth Airport the day after her landing at Londonderry, Ireland, on her flight from Harbor Grace, Nfld."

32. "The Society's Special Medal Awarded to Amelia Earhart," *National Geographic*, September 1932

Magazine spread: 14 x 10 in. (35.6 x 25.4 cm)
International Center of Photography, Museum Purchase

President Herbert Hoover presented Earhart the National Geographic Society's Medal on June 21, 1932. Commemorating the first medal awarded to a woman, the *National Geographic* article described Earhart's achievements.

33. Unidentified Photographer
Amelia Earhart and George Palmer Putnam, late May or early June 1932
Gelatin silver print
Image: 8 15/16 x 6 5/8 in. (22.7 x 16.8 cm); paper: 9 7/16 x 7 1/16 in. (24 x 17.9 cm)
International Center of Photography, The LIFE Magazine Collection

After a stop in London, Earhart continued on to Paris, the original destination of her cross-Atlantic flight. Putnam joined her there and accompanied her to Rome for meetings with Mussolini and the pope. Then they traveled to Brussels for lunch with the king and queen of Belgium.

34. "'Lady Lindy' Comes Home: Views of America's Reception for the First Woman to Fly the Atlantic Alone," *Mid-Week Pictorial*, July 2, 1932
Newspaper spread: 15 1/8 x 23 in. (38.4 x 58.4 cm)
International Center of Photography, Museum Purchase

With the 1932 flight, Earhart proved to herself and the public that she was a competent flyer and not just the passenger she had been in the 1928 *Friendship* crossing. "It always irked me

that the weather conditions were such that I couldn't do any of the piloting the other time I flew across. I didn't know enough about piloting to risk it. I thought that this would make up for that." Although she was greeted with parades and receptions in 1928, Earhart felt she truly deserved all of the excitement in 1932.

This spread from the July 2, 1932, *Mid-Week Pictorial* covered Earhart's ticker tape parade and adoring reception in New York City. For these public appearances, Earhart wore dresses or skirts (but none of the hats deemed "public menace[s]" and "cataclysms" by Putnam) rather than flight clothes.

35. Advertisement for Lucky Strike cigarettes, 1928
Offset lithography
11 5/8 x 8 9/16 in. (29.5 x 21.7 cm)
International Center of Photography, Museum Purchase

Putnam and Hilton Railey orchestrated Earhart's endorsement for Lucky Strike cigarettes. Featuring a drawing based on one of the photographs from the "Lady Lindy" series, the advertisement was an expeditious way for Earhart, a nonsmoker, to contribute $1,500 to Richard E. Byrd's Antarctica expedition. Byrd had helped catapult Earhart to fame; he served as technical advisor and made all of the arrangements for the *Friendship* flight. *McCall's*, which had asked Earhart to be a contributor to the magazine, found the advertisement "unladylike" and rescinded their offer.

36. Unidentified Photographer
Macy's window display on "Safety and

the Modern Air Liner," showcasing Amelia Earhart's luggage line, ca. 1933
Gelatin silver print
Image and paper: 7 7/8 x 9 7/16 in. (20 x 24 cm)
Courtesy of Purdue University Libraries, Archives & Special Collections [George Palmer Putnam Collection of Amelia Earhart Papers]

In addition to creating her own clothing line that was sold exclusively at Macy's, Earhart also endorsed a luggage line, which was manufactured by the Orenstein Trunk Corporation beginning in 1933. This waterproof luggage was made with lightweight material and designed to fit compactly into airplanes. Like most aviators of the day, Earhart was interested in creating a sense of "air-mindedness" in the American public that would encourage commercial aviation as a practical method of transportation.

37. "Designed by Amelia Earhart," *Woman's Home Companion*, August 1934
Photograph by Frederick Bradley
Magazine
13 3/4 x 10 7/8 x 1/8 in. (34.9 x 27.6 x 0.3 cm)
International Center of Photography, Museum Purchase

"Miss Earhart, you see, doesn't think of us as reclining Madame Récamiers. We may not pilot a plane, we may not play opposite Tilden on the courts, but we do lead active lives, nearly all of us. And so she has set herself the task of designing clothes to fit—simple comfortable clothes, free of all extraneous hangings even in the evening."

38. Advertisement for Eastman's Ciné-Kodak camera, 1933
Photographs of Amelia Earhart by Victor Keppler
Offset lithography
Spread: 12 11/16 x 19 in. (32.2 x 48.3 cm)
International Center of Photography, Museum Purchase

Presented as a story by Earhart about her travels and her "talent for being an eyewitness," this Kodak advertisement combines images of Earhart at home reading a book with ones of Earhart holding her plane's propeller. According to Earhart, pictures "are stabilizers on a shifting world and tend to keep records straight and memories fresh. The pleasure I might have felt as a child in having my picture taken has been somewhat dulled latterly through facing too many lenses. However, standing behind my own Ciné-Kodak directed at others is still a very real part of 'the fun of it'!"

39. Anton Bruehl
Amelia Earhart in a suit of her own design, 1934
For *Vogue* (June 1934)
Gelatin silver print
Image and paper: 10 1/4 x 8 1/4 in. (26 x 21 cm)
Courtesy Condé Nast Archives

A respected commercial photographer, Anton Bruehl photographed Earhart for a 1934 *Vogue* article that focused on the aviator's clothing line. Highlighting simple and elegant clothes for active, modern women, Earhart used unlikely fabrics and prints or accessories with subtle aviation motifs. Her creations, sold in Earhart's specialized boutiques

in major department stores in New York, Boston, and Chicago, were also available as patterns. These designs combined slim silhouettes and ease of movement. Although not revolutionary, they offered female consumers another way to identify with the famous flyer, who reportedly made her own outfits on occasion.

40. Frederick Bradley
Amelia Earhart with tailor and model, 1934
Gelatin silver print
Image and paper: 8 13/16 x 6 3/4 in. (22.4 x 17.1 cm)
International Center of Photography, The LIFE Magazine Collection

"Aviatrix Amelia Earhart's original interest in clothes designing consisted of cutting men's flying costumes down to fit her slim figure. Now, selling through stores all over the country, she announces a fifty-piece collection of sports clothes. Particularly she likes to use airplane fabrics and parachute silk, twist airplane engine parts into dress accessories."

Although Earhart did not design the clothes herself, she was actively involved in their production and made suggestions regarding colors and materials. For a variety of reasons, including the general economic depression, the line folded at the end of the year.

41. Frederick Bradley
Amelia Earhart in flying clothes of her own design, January 22, 1934
Gelatin silver print
Image and paper: 6 5/8 x 8 3/4 in. (16.8 x 22.2 cm)
The Schlesinger Library, Radcliffe Institute, Harvard University

In addition to designing clothing for modern women with active lifestyles, Earhart also designed flight clothes for her fellow female flyers. The slacks and windbreakers pictured here emphasized ease of movement but her real design innovation was a "monkey suit" with a zippered flap in the rear. Previously, women had to adapt men's flight suits so that they could easily relieve themselves on long-distance flights. Although Bradley took a series of pictures of Earhart in her creations, it appears that they were not the flying clothes she wore on any of her own record-breaking trips.

42. Unidentified Photographer
Amelia Earhart, January 4, 1935
Gelatin silver print
Image and paper: 8 7/8 x 6 15/16 in. (22.6 x 17.6 cm)
The Metropolitan Museum of Art, Purchase, Gap Foundation Gift, 1996 (1996.170)

In 1935, the Fashion Designers of America named Earhart one of the ten best-dressed women of the year. Earhart continued to refine her own sense of style and is seen here in her work clothes: a leather jacket, signature silk scarf, and khakis. Although Earhart was undoubtedly a role model for American women, Hollywood stars Katharine Hepburn and Marlene Dietrich were more responsible for making women's trousers fashionable and acceptable to the mainstream.

43. Unidentified Photographer
Amelia Earhart, 1932–36
Gelatin silver print
Image: 7 7/8 x 5 15/16 in. (20 x 15.1 cm); paper: 8 1/16 x 5 15/16 in. (20.5 x 15.1 cm)
The New York Times Photo Archives

Although similar in many ways to the picture discussed above, this image presents a more assertive Earhart. Rather than digging her hands into her pockets and tilting her head, Earhart stands up straight and looks directly at the camera. The softer, more feminine scarf has been replaced by a tie and the unstructured jacket has been exchanged for a leather bomber jacket.

44. Unidentified Photographer
Amelia Earhart, 1931
Gelatin silver print
Image and paper: 4 15/16 x 4 3/4 in. (12.5 x 12.1 cm)
International Center of Photography, The LIFE Magazine Collection

45. Unidentified Photographer
Amelia Earhart and George Palmer Putnam, May 29, 1931
Gelatin silver print
Image: 7 7/16 x 5 5/8 in. (18.9 x 14.3 cm); paper: 8 x 6 in. (20.3 x 15.2 cm)
International Center of Photography, The LIFE Magazine Collection

Putnam helps Earhart into her parachute at Newark before leaving on her cross-country trip in an autogiro, a plane that was invented in 1919. Called a "flying windmill" by the press, Earhart's autogiro was sponsored by the Beech-Nut Packing Company. She originally purchased the plane herself but sold it to the company and agreed to be a flying billboard for Beech-Nut. This was her second newsworthy event in an autogiro: the previous year, she became the first American woman to fly the plane.

46. Unidentified Photographer
Amelia Earhart in rubber lifeboat, 1935
Airbrushed gelatin silver print
Image and paper: 7 1/16 x 9 in. (17.9 x 22.9 cm)
International Center of Photography, The LIFE Magazine Collection

On January 11, 1935, Earhart set out to break another record—she would be the first person to fly solo from Hawaii to the U.S. mainland. Despite the success of the flight and the celebrated first use of a two-way radio in a nonmilitary plane, the press was disappointed with Earhart because she had accepted funding. Until the Hawaii flight, Putnam and Earhart had managed to finance her trips from donations and income from Earhart's books and lectures. This time, however, she had received $10,000 from the Hawaiian Sugar Planters' Association, which was fighting the tariff Congress had placed on its sugar.

Although this picture was taken before Earhart's Hawaii flight, it was repeatedly reproduced as an illustration of what she and navigator Fred Noonan might have had to use to survive if their plane crashed in the Pacific in 1937.

47. Unidentified Photographer
Amelia Earhart, Waikiki, Hawaii, 1935
Gelatin silver print
Image and paper: 8 1/8 x 10 in. (20.6 x 25.4 cm)
The Schlesinger Library, Radcliffe Institute, Harvard University

Earhart and Putnam were photographed in Hawaii visiting local celebrities, relaxing on the beach, eating pineapple, and listening to traditional music while bedecked in leis. Here Earhart, lounging in pants, pores over flight plans at the home of Christian and Mona Holmes in Waikiki. She also stayed with the Holmes during her 1937 flight and wrote her exclusive story of the trip from Oakland to Honolulu for the *New York Herald Tribune* there.

48. Unidentified Photographer
Amelia Earhart in Mexican dress, April 1935
Gelatin silver print
Image and paper: 2 1/2 x 1 3/4 in. (6.4 x 4.4 cm)
The Schlesinger Library, Radcliffe Institute, Harvard University

After her successful Hawaii flight, Earhart was invited by the Mexican government to fly to Mexico City as a good-will ambassador. She accepted the invitation and, on April 20, 1935, became the first person to fly from California to Mexico.

Although Earhart usually wore trousers in daily life, she generally wore simple yet elegantly tailored skirts and dresses for public occasions. When a similar image of Earhart appeared in the *New York Times*, a reader responded, "Yesterday I saw a newspaper picture of a lovely lady decked out in a Mexican sombrero and a striped serape. The caption read, 'Miss Earhart Goes Native.' Mexican women wear neither hats nor blankets. If a Mexican lady of high degree, visiting New York, dressed herself in overalls and a derby hat and paraded Fifth Avenue, the people back in Mexico would not believe she had

'gone native.' They would know she had gone crazy."

49. Unidentified Photographer
Diego Rivera and Amelia Earhart, April 1935
Gelatin silver print
Image and paper: 5 1/2 x 3 1/2 in. (14 x 9 cm)
Courtesy of Purdue University Libraries, Archives & Special Collections [George Palmer Putnam Collection of Amelia Earhart Papers]

A political progressive and advocate of women's rights, Earhart was vocal about her convictions. Perhaps it was she who initiated the visit with Rivera, an artist best known for the politically charged content of his murals.

50. Unidentified Photographer
Amelia Earhart, Mexico, April 1935
Gelatin silver print
Image and paper: 3 15/16 x 5 15/16 in. (10 x 15.1 cm)
The New York Times Photo Archives

"Amelia Earhart (Under the H) is quaintly entertained in Mexico before taking off for a non-stop attempt to New York."

51. Unidentified Photographer
Amelia Earhart, 1936
Gelatin silver print
Image and paper: 8 1/2 x 6 5/8 in. (21.6 x 16.8 cm)
International Center of Photography, The LIFE Magazine Collection

52. "When Ladies Take the Air," *Vanity Fair*, May 1932
Magazine
12 3/4 x 9 3/4 x 3/16 in. (32.4 x 24.8 x 0.5 cm)

International Center of Photography, Museum Purchase

Although Earhart was already planning her solo Atlantic crossing when this issue of *Vanity Fair* was published, she was not vocal about her plans. She appears here surrounded by other record-breaking female flyers, including Elinor Smith, Louise Thaden, Ruth Nichols, and Florence Lowe Barnes. Unlike these other women, Earhart was in possession of an adoring full-time publicist who was dedicated to marketing her image to the public: her husband.

53. Unidentified Photographer
Amelia Earhart, 1932
Gelatin silver print
Image: 9 1/2 x 7 1/2 in. (24.1 x 19.1 cm); paper: 10 x 8 in. (25.4 x 20.3 cm)
Courtesy Condé Nast Archives

Many pictures feature Earhart posed with her plane, seated in the cockpit, standing on the wing, or holding on to the propeller. It was during this period that people were especially interested in modernization, mechanization, and the speed of progress. In a very tangible way, Earhart, with her sleek and streamlined body type, short tousled hair, and mastery of the airplane, was a symbol of modernity. While many female aviators were often pictured with their planes, fashion models were also photographed with machinery.

54. Unidentified Photographer
Amelia Earhart and Melba Beard, August 31, 1935
Gelatin silver print
Image: 8 1/2 x 6 9/16 in. (21.6 x 16.7

cm); paper: 8 15/16 x 6 15/16 in. (22.7 x 17.6 cm)
The New York Times Photo Archives

The first National Air Races in 1929 featured the Women's Air Derby, disparagingly nicknamed "Powder Puff Air Derby." In 1935, the Earhart Prize, for which she donated the $1,250 purse, was won by Melba Beard, a twenty-two-year-old flyer who beat seven other pilots on the twenty-five-mile course. This photograph was used on the cover of the September 7, 1935, *Mid-Week Pictorial.*

55. Unidentified Photographer
Amelia Earhart surrounded by trophies, August 4, 1936
Gelatin silver print
Image: 6 1/16 x 7 15/16 in. (15.4 x 20.2 cm); paper: 6 1/2 x 8 7/16 in. (16.5 x 21.4 cm)
International Center of Photography, The LIFE Magazine Collection

"Amelia Earhart, famous flyer, will sponsor the feature Women's Handicap event in the 1936 National Air Races to open at Los Angeles September 4. The race for which Miss Earhart will present the trophy to the winner, will take place Sept. 5, and will include America's greatest feminine pilots. Miss Earhart is shown here with the trophies from which she will make her selection."

56. Unidentified Photographer
Mrs. Bernita S. Matthews, Mrs. Harvey W. Wiley, Amelia Earhart, Miss Anita Pollitzer, and Miss Ruth Taunton, menbers of the National Women's Party, White House, Washington, DC, September 22, 1932
Gelatin silver print

Image: 6 9/16 x 8 1/2 in. (16.7 x 21.6 cm); paper: 7 x 8 15/16 in. (17.8 x 22.7 cm)
The New York Times Photo Archives

"'Lady Lindy' joins in a plea for equal rights for women. Amelia Earhart (centre) calling at the White House with a delegation to present a petition of the National Women's Party."

Earhart actively promoted women's issues not only through her involvement with the National Women's Party but also in her magazine columns and lectures. She served as a role model of the New Woman in the United States, as well as a bridge between the suffragettes of the late nineteenth and early twentieth centuries and later feminists.

57. Unidentified Photographer
Amelia Earhart and Eleanor Roosevelt, April 30, 1933
Gelatin silver print
Image: 6 1/2 x 8 7/16 in. (16.5 x 21.4 cm); paper: 6 15/16 x 8 15/16 in. (17.6 x 22.7 cm)
The New York Times Photo Archives

"The pilot points out a path across the Potomac. Amelia Earhart, who after dinner at the White House took Mr. and Mrs. Roosevelt and eleven others as passengers in a plane piloted by her over Washington and Baltimore, talks with her distinguished passenger before the flight started."

Earhart and Roosevelt, two of the most famous public female figures in the United States in the 1930s, met in 1932 at one of the aviator's lectures and remained friends throughout Earhart's

life. Both of these politically progressive women were promoters of women's rights and aviation. Earhart had even offered to teach Roosevelt to fly, but FDR wouldn't allow it. Earhart and Putnam made numerous trips to the White House to visit with the Roosevelts and they relied heavily on these connections while finalizing the plans for Earhart's 1937 flight.

58. Unidentified Photographer
Amelia Earhart and students, February 26, 1933
Gelatin silver print
Image: 6 3/4 x 9 7/16 in. (16.1 x 24 cm); paper: 8 x 9 15/16 in. (20.3 x 25.2 cm)
The New York Times Photo Archives

"An authority encourages the youthful aeronauts: Mrs. Amelia Earhart Putnam advising boys of the aero model class of the Rye [NY] Y.M.C.A. on airplane construction on a visit to the clubhouse."

Although Earhart was primarily interested in using her fame to advance women's issues and highlight the need for girls and women to pursue their career goals, she also promoted aviation for all.

59. Unidentified Photographer
Amelia Earhart on her plane, July 21, 1936
Gelatin silver print
Image: 8 9/16 x 6 9/16 in. (21.8 x 16.7 cm); paper: 9 x 7 in. (22.9 x 17.8 cm)
The New York Times Photo Archives

"Amelia Earhart, 'Queen of the Air,' pictured astride the nose of her newly completed experimental Lockheed Electra flying laboratory built at a cost of $70,000, and which she will fly under the auspices of Purdue University, Indiana. The plane was put through its first test flight today at Union Air Terminal, Burbank, California. The two nine-cylinder, 550-horsepower Pratt & Whitney Wasp motors are seen in the above photo."

After working extensively with Lockheed in Burbank, California, to have the Electra made to her specifications (the passenger seats were replaced with additional fuel tanks, the instrument panel was redesigned, and a navigator's station was created), Earhart began planning for her most ambitious flight ever: a trip around the world at the equator. With her "flying laboratory," Earhart would "develop scientific and engineering data of vital importance to the aviation industry."

60. Unidentified Photographer
Amelia Earhart and Purdue University students Virginia Gardener, Rufinia Sexton, Barbara Sweeney, Betty Spilman, Barbara Cook, Louise Schickler, Mary Ed Johnston, Dorothy Hewitt, Gaby D. Roe, and Mary L. Hinchman, September 27, 1936
Gelatin silver print
Image: 7 5/8 x 9 1/2 in. (19.4 x 24.1 cm); paper: 8 1/16 x 10 in. (20.5 x 25.4 cm)
The New York Times Photo Archives

"The professor and some of her pupils in a new course at Purdue."

Edward C. Elliott, president of Purdue University, met Earhart at a panel discussion in 1934 and was immediately struck by her passion about the education and advancement of women. Although Earhart had no formal training as a teacher, Elliott invited her to consult at the university's new careers for women center in the fall of 1935. Earhart accepted the annual salary of $2,000 and spent time on the campus assisting women with their course selection and encouraging them to pursue their own careers. Although female students appreciated her, the conservative faculty and their wives objected to Earhart's presence and influence. Female student enrollment, however, increased by 50 percent.

61. Announcement of exclusive coverage of Amelia Earhart's 1937 flight, *New York Herald Tribune*, March 14, 1937
Newspaper
16 15/16 x 10 in. (43 x 25.4 cm)
International Center of Photography, Museum Purchase

As he had with Earhart's earlier record-breaking flights, Putnam arranged for exclusive coverage of the 1937 round-the-world trip. Over the course of the flight, the *New York Herald Tribune* published Earhart's daily dispatches.

62. Unidentified Photographer
Paul Mantz, Amelia Earhart, Harry Manning, and Fred Noonan with photographers, 1937
Gelatin silver print
Image and paper: 7 1/2 x 9 1/2 in. (19.1 x 24.1 cm)
Collection of Underwood Archives, Inc.

On the first attempt to make the 1937 flight, Earhart engaged two navigators: Harry Manning and Fred Noonan, in addition to Paul Mantz, who served as co-pilot and technical advisor. The flight was delayed after the Electra was damaged during takeoff in Hawaii in March 1937. This schedule change forced Manning to bow out due to prior job commitments. Earhart instead brought only Noonan, Pan Am's chief navigator, who had flown over the Pacific regularly.

63. Unidentified Photographer
Amelia Earhart showing the size of Howland Island, 1937
Gelatin silver print
Image: 8 1/2 x 6 1/2 in. (21.6 x 16.5 cm); paper: 9 1/8 x 7 in. (23.2 x 17.8 cm)
International Center of Photography, The LIFE Magazine Collection

This image was run after Earhart's disappearance: "Several months ago, when Amelia Earhart disclosed plans for her round-the-world flight, a reporter asked her how big Howland Island would look on the map compared to the other places she would visit, and she smilingly held up her hand as shown. Tonight [July 2, 1937] she apparently had missed the tiny island in her flight from New Guinea."

Earhart knew that the most difficult part of her round-the-world trip would be the 2,556-mile flight from Lae to Howland Island, a tiny speck in the South Pacific. In addition to building her a landing strip on the island with WPA funds, the U.S. government also stationed the USS *Ontario* midway between Lae and Howland and the Coast Guard cutter *Itasca* at Howland.

The *Itasca* was supposed to maintain radio contact with Earhart by issuing weather reports and sending up puffs of smoke to help guide her. Even though July 2, 1937, was a clear day, she never saw the smoke and she could make only sporadic radio contact.

64. Unidentified Photographer
Amelia Earhart at the controls of her Lockheed Electra, March 12, 1937
Gelatin silver print
Image: 8 9/16 x 6 13/16 in. (21.7 x 17.3 cm); paper: 9 x 7 in. (22.9 x 17.8 cm)
International Center of Photography, The LIFE Magazine Collection

"Amelia Earhart Putnam, conqueror by plane of both oceans, is poised at Oakland airport for the greatest air adventure of air history. She plans to be the first woman to circle the globe by plane, the greater part of which she will do alone. Highly pleased with preliminary tests, including blind flying, Amelia plans to hop off March 15, her first stopover at Honolulu."

Earhart described the cramped conditions of the Electra's cockpit: it was only "four feet six inches by four feet six inches." The bamboo pole along the roof was used for passing notes back to Noonan. The circular object on top is Earhart's Bendix radio direction finder. She and Noonan jettisoned their marine frequency radio and trailing antenna because neither was proficient with Morse code. These devices might have helped them locate Howland Island.

65. Unidentified Photographer
Amelia Earhart and her Lockheed Electra above the Golden Gate Bridge, March 17, 1937
Gelatin silver print

Image: 7 1/2 x 9 7/16 in. (19.1 x 24 cm); paper: 8 1/16 x 9 11/16 in. (20.5 x 24.6 cm)
International Center of Photography, The LIFE Magazine Collection

66. Unidentified Photographer
Amelia Earhart and George Palmer Putnam, May 29, 1937
Gelatin silver print
Paper: 8 x 10 in. (20.3 x 25.4 cm)
Time, Inc. Picture Collection

"Amelia Earhart Putnam, famous flyer, and her publisher husband, George Palmer Putnam, talk over plans for the aviatrix's second attempt to fly around the world. They are chatting in a hanger [in Miami, Florida] where Mrs. Putnam's plane is being prepared for the flight."

Earhart had planned to fly west around the world, but her plane was damaged during takeoff from Hawaii on March 20, 1937. The plane was returned to the Lockheed plant in California for $14,000 in repairs, an expense that necessitated further fundraising. Earhart had autographed and sold 10,000 envelopes with airmail stamps to pay for the flight, but she and Putnam also needed to ask friends for money. According to Earhart, they "mortgaged the future" to finance the trip.

67. Unidentified Photographer
Amelia Earhart and George Palmer Putnam, June 1, 1937
Gelatin silver print
Image: 8 7/16 x 6 3/4 in. (21.4 x 17.1 cm); paper: 9 x 7 1/8 in. (22.9 x 18.1 cm)
International Center of Photography, The LIFE Magazine Collection

"George Palmer Putnam bids his wife, Mrs. Amelia Earhart goodbye and good luck before her departure here this morning at 5:57 A.M. on her second attempt to fly around the world, accompanied by only Capt. Fred Noonan. She headed for San Juan, Puerto Rico, a 1,181-mile non-stop hop and first leg of the journey in her twin-motored Lockheed monoplane, carrying 600 gallons of gasoline for the approximately 7-hour trip."

Reversing traditional gender roles, Earhart left Putnam at home while she went on trips. This was the last time they saw each other. When Earhart and Noonan failed to reach Howland Island, Putnam and Noonan's wife waited in San Francisco for news. U.S. ships combed the area around Howland for seventeen days; no traces of the plane or its inhabitants were ever found.

68. Unidentified Photographer
Amelia Earhart and Fred Noonan, June 8, 1937
Gelatin silver print
Image: 7 13/16 x 6 1/16 in. (19.8 x 15.4 cm); paper: 8 7/16 x 6 9/16 in. (21.4 x 16.7 cm)
International Center of Photography, The LIFE Magazine Collection

"Miss Amelia Earhart and her navigator Fred Noonan are pictured at the airport here [Dakar, Senegal] as they studied a map of the route over the jungle to Niamey, French West Africa [now Niger], 1,275 miles east of this point. Miss Earhart set her fleet twin-motored Lockheed Electra down on Dakar airport on June 8, the day after she landed at St. Louis, 163 miles north, following a flight across the South Atlantic from

Natal, Brazil. She and Captain Noonan are making a leisurely flight around the world at its 'waist.'"

69. Unidentified Photographer
Amelia Earhart and Fred Noonan in Natal, Brazil, June 18, 1937
Gelatin silver print
Image: 8 5/8 x 5 7/8 in. (21.9 x 14.9 cm); paper: 9 1/16 x 7 in. (23 x 17.8 cm)
International Center of Photography, The LIFE Magazine Collection

70. Unidentified Photographer
Amelia Earhart with camera, late June 1937
Gelatin silver print
Image and paper: 7 15/16 x 5 15/16 in. (20.2 x 15.1 cm)
International Center of Photography, The LIFE Magazine Collection

"One of the last pictures taken of Mrs. Amelia Earhart Putnam before she took off from New Guinea for her ill-fated flight to Howland Island."

While living in Los Angeles in 1923, Earhart worked in a photography studio; she and a friend later briefly operated their own photography business. This interest endured; Earhart took a number of photographs of clouds and ships that passed below as the *Friendship* crossed the Atlantic in 1928 and she continued to take pictures of the people and places she visited. These pictures from 1937, along with diary entries that she was writing for the book about her flight, were mailed back to Putnam in the United States.

71. Unidentified Photographer
Amelia Earhart and Fred Noonan, late June 1937

Gelatin silver print
Image: 8 3/8 x 6 5/8 in. (21.3 x 16.8 cm); paper: 9 1/16 x 6 15/16 in. (23 x 17.6 cm)
International Center of Photography, The LIFE Magazine Collection

"Amelia Earhart and her navigator, Fred Noonan, are shown resting beside their plane here [Batavia, Dutch East Indies, now Jakarta, Indonesia] before the round-the-world flight which ended when they were forced to land on the Pacific near Howland Island. This picture, sent by radio from London to New York, is believed to be the last taken of the pair before their mid-ocean disaster."

Earhart and Noonan did sightsee in Jakarta, but this image was probably taken in Bandung, three hours away. The pair spent six days in Bandung, a hub for KLM's South Pacific flights. KLM's mechanics made a number of repairs on the Electra before Earhart and Noonan flew on to Surabaja on June 26, 1937.

72. Page from Amelia Earhart's *Last Flight*, 1937
Book
8 3/16 x 5 5/8 x 1 1/4 in. (20.8 x 14.3 x 3.2 cm)
Collection of Ann L. Morse

Published by Putnam after Earhart's disappearance, *Last Flight* presents the aviator's chronicle of preparations for the 1937 flight. The book also includes Earhart's diary entries written during the flight, images she took, and extensive commentary by Putnam.

73. Albert L. Bresnik
Amelia Earhart in front of a map

showing the route for her flight, 1937
Gelatin silver print
Image and paper: 9 1/16 x 7 1/2 in. (23 x 19 cm)
Courtesy of Purdue University Libraries, Archives & Special Collections [George Palmer Putnam Collection of Amelia Earhart Papers]

In an attempt to control the circulation of images of Earhart, Putnam named Albert L. Bresnik the flyer's "official photographer." This image was used as the cover for *Last Flight*.

74. Dick Whittington
Amelia Earhart, 1935, *Los Angeles Times*, July 18, 1937
Newspaper
21 15/16 x 15 9/16 in. (55.7 x 39.5 cm)
International Center of Photography, Museum Purchase

"She was not afraid!" reads the ink inscription on this newspaper rotogravure that ran after Earhart and Noonan disappeared. Many of Earhart's fans, especially female ones, collected images of her and wrote moving letters to Earhart's mother about the flyer's impact on their lives.

75. Page of Amy Otis Earhart's scrapbook, 1937
14 x 10 3/4 in. (35.6 x 27.3 cm)
The Schlesinger Library, Radcliffe Institute, Harvard University

Earhart's mother, Amy Otis Earhart, kept a scrapbook of her daughter's final flight and the aftermath. In the absence of post-disappearance photos, illustrators created images such as "The Universal Question" and others that showed Earhart seated on the nose of her plane in the middle of the ocean.

76. Page of Amy Otis Earhart's scrapbook, 1939
Photograph of Amelia Earhart by Ben Pinchot
14 x 10 3/4 in. (35.6 x 27.3 cm)
The Schlesinger Library, Radcliffe Institute, Harvard University

Earhart, dressed in a trench coat and silk scarf, radiates calm as she gazes intently at the viewer. This portrait, supposedly taken days before Earhart left for her 1937 flight, was often reproduced in tributes to her. One syndicated newspaper chain ran this photograph along with pictures of the Lockheed Electra and Fred Noonan, a map of the flight path, and a map showing Howland Island.

The extensive search was called off on July 19, 1937, and Earhart was declared legally dead on January 5, 1939.

77. "Log of Earhart's 'Last Stunt Flight,'" *Life*, July 19, 1939
Magazine spread: 14 x 21 in. (35.6 x 53.3 cm)
International Center of Photography, Museum Purchase

After her disappearance, many magazines and periodicals published tributes to Earhart, often accompanied by photo essays containing highlights of her career. Although her courage was praised and her accomplishments acknowledged as beneficial to women, *Life* and other magazines viewed Earhart's 1937 flight as a "stunt" that had done more harm than good to the burgeoning aviation industry. "As the

world's worried eyes were fixed on the Pacific and the Earhart search, a far more important aviation event was taking place quietly over the mid-Atlantic, the first of a series of survey flights which are expected to lead . . . to the establishment of airmail service to Europe and . . . of the first trans-Atlantic passenger service."

78. "World Remembers," *Los Angeles Herald and Express*, July 13, 1937
Newspaper
21 1/2 x 16 1/2 in. (54.6 x 41.9 cm)
The Schlesinger Library, Radcliffe Institute, Harvard University

79. Unidentified Photographer
Twenty-foot snow statue of Amelia Earhart, Virginia, Minnesota, February 1938
Gelatin silver print postcard
Image: 3 1/8 x 5 1/8 in. (7.9 x 13 cm); paper: 3 7/16 x 5 7/16 in. (8.7 x 13.8 cm)
International Center of Photography, Museum Purchase

Earhart's disappearance, discussed throughout the world, prompted ephemeral and fantastic tributes, such as this snow sculpture.

80. Unidentified Photographer
Amelia Earhart on the wing of her plane, 1937/1945
Gelatin silver print
Image: 7 11/16 x 9 1/2 in. (19.5 x 24.1 cm); paper: 8 3/16 x 10 in. (20.8 x 25.4 cm)
International Center of Photography, The LIFE Magazine Collection

According to the inscription on the back of this photograph, the picture

was removed from a "dead Jap" in Okinawa during World War II. It was intended to prove that Earhart and Noonan had contact with the Japanese. One theory, first introduced in the 1943 film *Flight for Freedom* and later elaborated in the 1970 book *Amelia Earhart Lives*, is that Earhart had been a spy for the U.S. government and that she had flown into Japanese territory so that the U.S. would have access to the area to make accurate maps of the Pacific islands. Another theory suggested that the flyers had landed on Mili Atoll after missing Howland Island and were taken to Saipan by the Japanese. Two Japanese battleships were in the area on July 2, but neither ship's log records seeing the Electra or rescuing the flyers.

81. Unidentified Photographer
Amelia Earhart at a Japanese tea ceremony, Hawaii, 1935/1970
Gelatin silver print
Image: 7 1/2 x 9 11/16 in. (19.1 x 24.6cm); paper: 8 x 19 1/16 in. (20.3 x 25.6.8 cm)
The New York Times Photo Archives

This photograph appears in *Amelia Earhart Lives*. It is captioned: "Kimono-clad Amelia Earhart (center) being served tea in a Japanese tearoom. This unique photo was planted and recently found in Joe Gervais' safe." In publicity material, the publishers point out that Earhart had not visited Japan prior to her disappearance in 1937. Klaas says that the Japanese setting had been authenticated by "a scholar who lived in Japan" and "a recognized analyst of photographs."

The photograph was actually taken during Earhart's 1935 trip to Hawaii.

82. Unidentified Photographer
Irene Bolam, 1970
Gelatin silver print
Image: 9 3/8 x 7 11/16 in. (23.8 x 19.5 cm); paper: 9 15/16 x 8 1/16 in. (25.2 x 20.5 cm)
The New York Times Photo Archives

Because the bodies of Earhart and Noonan were never found, conspiracy theories emerged in the following years. In *Amelia Earhart Lives* (1970), Joe Klaas, working with Joe Gervais, claimed that Earhart had been a spy sent to photograph the islands of the Pacific, and was living in the United States as Irene Bolam after surviving the 1937 crash. Bolam, a pilot who, like Earhart, was a member of the Ninety-Nines and Zonta, ferociously denied the allegation to the press and eventually sued Gervais to end his harassment of her.

83. *Ms.*, September 1976
Magazine
10 13/16 x 8 3/16 x 1/8 in. (27.5 x 20.8 x 0.3 cm)
International Center of Photography, Museum Purchase

Although conspiracy theories kept Earhart in the press for decades after her disappearance, it was the women's movement of the 1970s that reclaimed Earhart as a feminist icon and role model for women and girls. This issue of *Ms.* declared that Earhart was "better than the myth."

84. Advertisement for Gap khakis, 1993
Offset lithography
10 7/16 x 8 1/8 in. (26.5 x 20.6 cm)
International Center of Photography, Museum Purchase

In 1993, the Gap launched an advertising campaign of famous people from the past wearing khakis. Rather than wearing khakis as part of a conformist uniform, the consumer would be in the company of such iconic trailblazers as Marlene Dietrich, James Dean, Marilyn Monroe, Picasso, Andy Warhol, and Frank Lloyd Wright.

85. Advertisement for Apple Inc., 1998
Offset lithography
17 1/8 x 11 in. (43.5 x 27.9 cm)
International Center of Photography, Museum Purchase

Apple's 1998 "Think Different" campaign also used images of famous people to sell their computer products. The television commercials paid homage to "the crazy ones. The misfits. The rebels.... The ones who see things differently. They're not fond of rules. And they have no respect for the status quo. You can praise them, disagree with them, quote them, disbelieve them, glorify or vilify them. About the only thing that you can't do is ignore them." Apple's products, the ads suggest, are designed for those contemporary creative people who ignore boundaries, just as Albert Einstein, John Lennon and Yoko Ono, Buckminster Fuller, Picasso, Martha Graham, Alfred Hitchcock, and Jim Henson did.

The print ads rely on the viewer's recognition of the celebrity; the subject's name is never given. Earhart's unique image continues to suggest flight, adventure, glamour, and daring to each generation.

Selected Bibliography

The literature on Amelia Earhart is vast, and much of it addresses disappearance theories and other topics outside the scope of this book. What follows is a selected list of sources that are most relevant to an examination of the construction and reception of Earhart's public image.

Earhart, Amelia. "When Women Go Aloft." *The Bostonian* (May 1928), pp. 5–6.

"A Woman Hops the Atlantic." *The Literary Digest,* June 30, 1928, pp. 8–9.

Earhart, Amelia. "This Boston." *The Bostonian* (July 1928), p. 3.

___. "Try Flying Yourself." *Cosmopolitan* (November 1928), pp. 32–35, 158–60.

McIntyre, O. O. "I Want You to Meet a Real American Girl." *Cosmopolitan* (November 1928), p. 21.

Earhart, Amelia. "What Miss Earhart Thinks When She's Flying: An Intimate Article Written While She Was Vagabonding by Air." *Cosmopolitan* (December 1928), pp. 28–29, 195–96.

___. "Miss Earhart Answers Some Questions About Flying." *Cosmopolitan* (December 1928), pp. 30–31, 195.

___. *20 Hrs. 40 Min.: Our Flight in the Friendship. The American Girl, First Across the Atlantic by Air, Tells Her Story.* New York and London: G. P. Putnam's Sons, 1928.

___. "Here Is How Fannie Hurst Could Learn to Fly." *Cosmopolitan* (January 1929), pp. 56–57, 163–64.

___. "Is It Safe for You to Fly?" *Cosmopolitan* (February 1929), pp. 90–91, 148.

___. "Shall You Let Your Daughter Fly?" *Cosmopolitan* (March 1929), pp. 88–89, 142–43.

___. "Clouds." *Cosmopolitan* (April 1929), pp. 86–87.

___. "The Man Who Tells the Flier: 'Go!'" *Cosmopolitan* (May 1929), pp. 78–79, 144, 146.

___. "Why Are Women Afraid to Fly?" *Cosmopolitan* (July 1929), pp. 70–71, 138, 140.

___. "Fly America First." *Cosmopolitan* (October 1929), pp. 80–81, 134–36.

___. "Miss Earhart's Adventure on the Floor of the Sea." *Cosmopolitan* (November 1929), pp. 45, 98, 100, 101.

___. "Mrs. Lindbergh." *Cosmopolitan* (July 1930), pp. 78–79, 196–97.

Markey, Morris. "Young Man of Affairs–I." *New Yorker,* September 20, 1930, pp. 26–32.

___. "Young Man of Affairs–II." *New Yorker,* September 27, 1930, pp. 30–33.

Earhart, Amelia. "Mother Reads as We Fly." *Cosmopolitan* (January 1931), p. 17.

___. "Your Next Garage May House an Autogiro." *Cosmopolitan* (August 1931), pp. 58–59, 160–61.

___. "Flying the Atlantic—and selling sausage have a lot of things in common." *The American Magazine* (August 1932), pp. 15–16, 72.

___. "Flying Is Fun!" *Cosmopolitan* (August 1932), pp. 38–39.

___. "Women and Courage." *Cosmopolitan* (September 1932), pp. 54–55, 147–48.

___. "My Flight from Hawaii." *National Geographic* (September 1932), pp. 593–609.

The Nation, September 7, 1932, p. 202.

Earhart, Amelia. "Forgotten Husband G. P. Putnam." *Pictorial Review* (December 1932), pp. 12–13.

___. *The Fun of It: Random Records of My Own Flying and of Women in Aviation*. New York: Brewer, Warren & Putnam, 1932.

___. "First Lady of the Sky." *Vogue*, January 15, 1933, pp. 30–31, 66.

___. "Part of Fun of It." *House and Garden* (April 1933), pp. 62–63.

"Sticky Business." *The Nation*, January 30, 1935, p. 118.

"EARHART: Good-Will Emissary Again Achieves the Unusual." *Newsweek*, May 18, 1935, pp. 34–35.

"The Society's Special Medal Awarded to Amelia Earhart: First Woman to Receive Geographic Distinction at Brilliant Ceremony in the National Capital." *National Geographic* (May 1935), pp. 358–66.

"Search Abandoned." *Time*, July 12, 1937, p. 36.

"Lost Earhart." *Time*, July 12, 1937, pp. 50–51.

"A Round-The-World Flight Ends in the Pacific." *Life*, July 19, 1937, pp. 21–23.

"Transport." *Time*, July 19, 1937, pp. 45–46.

Boykin, Elizabeth MacRae. "Amelia Earhart at Home." *Better Homes and Gardens* (February 1937), pp. 46–47.

"A.E." *Aviation* 36, no. 8 (August 1937), p. 22.

Earhart, Amelia. *Last Flight*. New York: Harcourt, Brace, 1937.

Putnam, George Palmer. *Soaring Wings: A Biography of Amelia Earhart*. New York: Harcourt, Brace, 1939.

Wecter, Dixon. *The Hero in America: A Chronicle of Hero–Worship*. Ann Arbor: University of Michigan Press, 1963.

Trahey, Jane, ed. *Harper's Bazaar: 100 Years of the American Female*. New York: Random House, 1967.

Freedman, Estelle B. "The New Woman: Changing Views of Women in the 1920s." *Journal of American History* 61 (September 1974), pp. 372–93.

Corn, Joseph J. "Making Flying 'Thinkable': Women Pilots and the Selling of Aviation, 1927–1940." *American Quarterly* 31, no. 4 (1979), pp. 556–71.

Ware, Susan. *Holding Their Own: American Women in the 1930s*. Boston: Twayne, 1982.

Brown, Dorothy M. *Setting a Course: American Women in the 1920s*. Boston: Twayne, 1987.

Lovell, Mary S. *The Sound of Wings: The Life of Amelia Earhart*. New York: St. Martin's Press, 1989.

Rich, Doris L. *Amelia Earhart: A Biography*. Washington, DC: Smithsonian Institution Press, 1989.

McGerr, Michael. "Political Style and Women's Power, 1830–1930." *Journal of American History* 77 (December 1990), pp. 864–85.

Ardis, Ann L. *New Women, New Novels: Feminism and Early Modernism*. New Brunswick, NJ: Rutgers University Press, 1990.

Cadogan, Mary. *Women with Wings: Female Flyers in Fact and Fiction*. Chicago: Academy Chicago, 1992.

Ware, Susan. "Amelia Earhart as Popular Heroine." *Culturefront* (Fall 1993), pp. 10–13.

___. *Still Missing: Amelia Earhart and the Search for Modern Feminism*. New York: W. W. Norton, 1993.

Kenney, Keith R., and Brent W. Unger. "*The Mid-Week Pictorial*: Forerunner of American News-Picture Magazines." *American Journalism* 11, no. 3 (1994), pp. 242–56.

Jay, Karla. "No Bumps, No Excrescences: Amelia Earhart's Failed Flight into Fashions." In *On Fashion*, edited by Shari Benstock and Suzanne Ferriss. New Brunswick, NJ: Rutgers University Press, 1994.

Ponce de Leon, Charles L. "The Man Nobody Knows: Charles A. Lindbergh and the Culture of Celebrity." *Prospects* 21 (1996), pp. 347–72.

Millward, Liz. "The 'Aerial Eye': Gender and the Colonization of Airspace." *Michigan Feminist Studies* 13 (1998–99), pp. 1–18.

Telotte, J. P. "Lindbergh, Film, and Machine Age Dreams." *South Atlantic Review* 64, no. 4 (1999), pp. 68–83.

Butler, Susan. *East to the Dawn: The Life of Amelia Earhart.* New York: Da Capo Press, 1999.

Kitch, Carolyn. "Destructive Women and Little Men: Masculinity, the New Woman, and Power in 1910s Popular Media." *Journal of Magazine & New Media Research* (Northwestern University) 1, no. 1 (1999), at http://www.bsu.edu/web/aejmcmagazine/journal/archive/Spring_1999/article1.html

Smith, Sidonie. "Virtually Modern Amelia: Mobility, Flight, and the Discontents of Identity." In *Virtual Gender: Fantasies of Subjectivity and Embodiment,* edited by Mary Ann O'Farrell and Lynne Vallone. Ann Arbor: University of Michigan Press, 1999.

Herrmann, Anne. "Amelia Earhart: The Aviatrix as American Dandy." In her *Queering the Moderns,* pp. 14–39. New York: Palgrave Macmillan, 2000.

Swinth, Kirsten. "Categorizing the Female Type: Images of Women as Symbols of Historical Change." *Reviews in American History* 30 (December 2002), pp. 604–13.

Kitch, Carolyn. *The Girl on the Magazine Cover: The Origins of Visual Stereotypes in American Mass Media.* Chapel Hill: University of North Carolina Press, 2001.

Smith, Sidonie. *Moving Lives: Twentieth-Century Women's Travel Writing.* Minneapolis: University of Minnesota Press, 2001.

Wosk, Julie. *Women and the Machine: Representations from the Spinning Wheel to the Electronic Age.* Baltimore: Johns Hopkins University Press, 2001.

Piper, Karen Lynnea. "The Gendered Aerial Perspective." In her *Cartographic Fictions: Maps, Race, and Identity.* New Brunswick, NJ: Rutgers University Press, 2002.

Ponce de Leon, Charles L. *Self-Exposure: Human-Interest Journalism and the Emergence of Celebrity in America, 1890–1940.* Chapel Hill: University of North Carolina Press, 2002.

Matthews, Jean V. *The Rise of the New Woman: The Women's Movement in America, 1875–1930.* Chicago: Ivan R. Dee, 2003.

Wohl, Robert. *The Spectacle of Flight: Aviation and the Western Imagination, 1920–1950.* New Haven: Yale University Press, 2005.

INTERNATIONAL CENTER OF PHOTOGRAPHY

Published in conjunction with the exhibition *Amelia Earhart: Image and Icon* organized by the International Center of Photography, New York

Exhibition Dates: May 11 through September 9, 2007

This exhibition was organized by the International Center of Photography and made possible with support from Ann L. Morse, Frank and Mary Ann Arisman, Thomas L. Chrystie, Andrew and Marina Lewin, and other donors.

First edition 2007

Copublished by the International Center of Photography, New York, and Steidl Publishers, Göttingen, Germany

Director of Publications: Karen Hansgen
Editors: Kristen Lubben; Erin Barnett
Copyeditor: Philomena Mariani
Design: Claas Möller, Steidl Design
Separations: Steidl's digital darkroom
Production: Steidl, Göttingen

International Center of Photography

1114 Avenue of the Americas
New York, NY 10036
www.icp.org

STEIDL

Düstere Str. 4 / D–37073 Göttingen
Phone +49 551-49 60 60 / Fax +49 551-49 60 649
E-mail: mail@steidl.de

ISBN
Printed in Germany

cover: Unidentified Photographer, Amelia Earhart, 1936
back cover: Unidentified Photographer, Amelia Earhart's first parachute drop, June 1935
frontispiece: Jake Coolidge, Amelia Earhart, from the "Lady Lindy" series, June 1928 (The New York Times Photo Archives)
page 8: Unidentified Photographer, Amelia Earhart, 1926 (The Schlesinger Library, Radcliffe Institute, Harvard University)
page 24: Unidentified Photographer, Amelia Earhart, May 22, 1932
page 32: Unidentified Photographer, Amelia Earhart and Fred Noonan, late June 1937
pages 166-167: Amelia Earhart, Clouds, June 1928 (The New York Times Photo Archives)